INSTA GRAPHICS

D1470379

A VISUAL GUIDE TO YOUR UNIVERSE

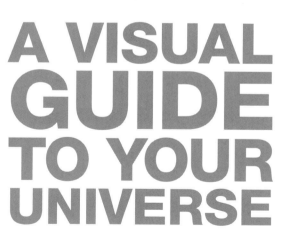

DAN GREEN

SCHOLASTIC

Library of Congress Cataloging-in-Publication Data available

ISBN 978-1-338-21557-1

10 9 8 7 6 5 4 3 2 1   19 20 21 22 23

Printed in the U.S.A. 40
First edition 2019

This book was created and produced by
Toucan Books Limited
Text: Dan Green
Designer: Lee Riches
Editor: Anna Southgate
Proofreader: Marion Dent
Index: Marie Lorimer
Picture research: Lee Riches and
Sharon Southren

CONTENTS

HOME SWEET HOME

HERE WE ARE. THIS IS OUR HOME IN SPACE—PLANET EARTH. NO ONE HAD SEEN THIS VIEW OF EARTH UNTIL THE 1960S, WHEN HUMANS BEGAN TO TRAVEL INTO SPACE; THEY LOOKED BACK AND SAW THIS AMAZING SIGHT.

Earth is the third planet from the sun.

Our planet travels at 67,000 MPH (108,000 kmh) around the sun.

It is 4.5 billion years old.

13,170,000,000,000,000,000,000,000 lb
(5,972,000,000,000,000,000,000,000 kg) weight

Earth is the only
planet with life (so far

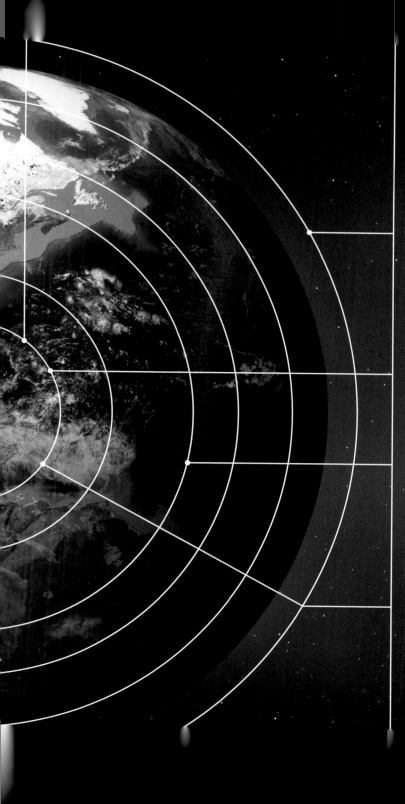

The temperature rises 1°F (0.6°C) for every 70 ft (20 m) of depth inside the planet.

A 300-mile-thick (480 km) layer of gas—the atmosphere—surrounds Earth, most of it within 10 miles (16 km) of its surface.

Earth is 24,901 miles (40,075 km) around its middle.

Some 71% of Earth's surface is covered by liquid water and 29% by land.

It is 3,960 miles (6,373 km) to the center of the Earth.

Just 2.5% of Earth's water is fresh, and

WACKY WORLD
CHAPTER 1

DID YOU KNOW?

Monarch butterflies migrate thousands of miles each year to survive cold winter temperatures. Dragonflies migrate, too. Which insect do you think travels the farthest, and how far could they possibly go? Turn to page **24** to find out!

HIGHEST MOUNTAINS

ALL OF THE WORLD'S HIGHEST MOUNTAINS ARE IN THE HIMALAYAS AND THE KARAKORAM—14 PEAKS OVER 26,247 FT (8,000 M). THE CONTINENTS EACH HAVE THEIR OWN HIGHEST PEAK, AS WELL AS A HANDFUL WORTHY OF A SPECIAL MENTION.

WORLD #1
(also Asia #1): Everest
(29,035 ft / 8,850 m)

N. AMERICA #1:
Denali
(20,310 ft / 6,190 m)

ANTARCTICA #1:
Vinson Massif
(16,050 ft / 4,892 m)

MONT BLANC
(15,777 ft / 4,809 m)
Highest peak in the Alps

FUJI
(12,388 ft / 3,776 m)
Highest mountain in Japan

KOSCIUSZKO
(7,310 ft / 2,228 m)
Highest mountain in Australia

K2
(28,251 ft / 8,611 m)
Climbers face the
challenge of frequent,
savage storms

ANNAPURNA 1
(26,545 ft / 8,091 m)
The world's deadliest
mountain

S. AMERICA #1:
Aconcagua
(22,831 ft / 6,959 m)
Has two summits for
climbers to scale—north
and south

AFRICA #1:
Kilimanjaro
(19,340 ft / 5,895 m)

EUROPE #1:
Elbrus
(18,510 ft / 5,642 m)

OCEANIA #1:
Puncak Jaya
(16,024 ft / 4,884 m)

MAUNA KEA
(13,796 ft / 4,205 m)
World's tallest mountain
measured from its base on
the seafloor (about
33,500 ft / 10,210 m tall)

WASHINGTON
(6,288 ft / 1,917 m)
Held the world's strongest
wind record for 62 years—
231 MPH (372 kmh)

 WHAT MAKES A MOUNTAIN?
Mountain ranges form when Earth's
tectonic plates collide. Fifty million years ago, the
Indian continental plate smashed into the Eurasian
continental plate. As these lumbering landmasses
drove into each other, the Indian plate crumpled
and was pushed underneath Asia, lifting the
land to create the newest mountain range on
the planet—the Himalayas.

Saharan Desert

Great Basin Desert

Patagonian Desert

LARGEST DESERTS

DESERTS ARE BONE-DRY PLACES THAT RECEIVE ALMOST NO RAIN. THEY COVER ABOUT ONE-THIRD OF THE EARTH'S LAND SURFACE, BUT NOT ALL ARE LIFELESS SAND DUNES. HERE ARE THE TOP TEN DRIEST PLACES ON THE PLANET.

GREAT BASIN DESERT
Temperate desert
190,000 sq mi (492,000 km²)
This desert has hot, dry summers and snowy winters. It is home to the world's oldest living things—the bristlecone pines—and is known for its dried-up salt lakes. Animals that live here include the bighorn sheep and the desert horned lizard.

PATAGONIAN DESERT
Neotropical desert
188,100 sq mi (488,177 km²)
Ravaged by a fierce westerly wind, the Patagonian Desert is a harsh environment. Nevertheless, people use it to raise sheep. It is also home to diverse, unique wildlife, such as the guanaco (related to the llama), puma, Patagonian fox, and lesser rhea.

SAHARAN DESERT
Subtropical, hot desert
3,320,000 sq mi (8,600,000 km²)
Covering most of northern Africa, the Sahara is nearly as large as the United States. It has some of the largest sand dunes in the world, including some giants that peak at 590 ft (180 m) tall. Among the animals that live here are fennec foxes and jackals.

Arctic

Gobi Desert

Arabian Desert

Great Victoria Desert

Kalahari Desert

Antarctica

 ## WHAT MAKES A DESERT?

Deserts are dry regions that receive less than 10 in (25 cm) of rainfall a year. Typically, they have very little vegetation. Plants and animals that live there are adapted to survive in harsh, arid environments.

ARCTIC
Polar desert

62,300 sq mi (161,400 km²)
Go as far north as you can and you'll encounter the Arctic Desert. The Arctic is a vast ocean covered in winter sea ice and permafrost tundra, roamed by caribou, arctic fox, seals, and polar bears.

GOBI DESERT
Rain-shadow desert

500,000 sq mi (1,300,000 km²)
Famous for its dinosaur fossils, the largest desert region in Asia is largely exposed bare rock whipped by high winds. Vast Himalayan mountain peaks block rain clouds from reaching the Gobi Desert. Among the animals living here are the endangered Gobi bear and the Gobi viper.

ARABIAN DESERT
Subtropical, hot desert

900,000 sq mi (2,300,000 km²)
Crisscrossed by camel trails, the Arabian Desert covers most of the Arabian Peninsula. At its baking heart is the world's largest area of continuous sand—Rub' al-Khali, or the Empty Quarter.

KALAHARI DESERT
Semiarid savanna

360,000 sq mi (930,000 km²)
Although some regions of the Kalahari receive as much as 10 in (25 cm) annual rainfall, sectors of it are still true desert. Meerkats, springbok, and wildcats roam the land here, and it is home to the world's second-largest protected area.

ANTARCTICA
Polar desert

5,400,000 sq mi (14,000,000 km²)
At about 1.5 times the size of the United States, Earth's southernmost continent is almost entirely encased in ice. The 1.2-mi-thick (2 km) ice cap contains 90 percent of the world's ice and 70 percent of the world's fresh water. Penguins and seals live here.

GREAT VICTORIA DESERT
Subtropical, hot desert

161,680 sq mi (418,750 km²)
With 10 different deserts, Australia is the driest continent on Earth after Antarctica. Although the Great Victoria Desert receives very little rainfall, it is covered in vegetation and is home to lots of wildlife, including more than 100 species of reptiles.

HAILSTONES

STINGING SHOWERS HAMMER DOWN FROM THE SKY SHATTERING GLASS, DENTING CARS, AND HARMING LIVESTOCK. HAIL SIZES RANGE FROM PUNY PEA-SIZED PELLETS TO MONSTERS THE SIZE OF SOFTBALLS. RUN FOR COVER!

PEA
¼ in (0.6 cm)

MARBLE
½ in (1.3 cm)

PING-PONG BALL
1½ in (3.8 cm)

GOLF BALL
1¾ in (4.45 cm)

TENNIS BALL
2½ in (6.35 cm)

BASEBALL
2¾ in (7 cm)

 HOW HAILSTONES FORM

Hail forms inside tall storm clouds. Updrafts carry raindrops high into the atmosphere, where they freeze into solid balls of ice. Typically, inside a thundercloud, strong updrafts lift hailstones to the top of the cloud. Each time a frozen drop makes a loop, it picks up a new layer of ice and grows bigger. Eventually, the hailstone is too large to be lifted by the updraft and it falls to Earth as hail.

SOFTBALL
4½ in (11.4 cm)

AFRICAN BUSH ELEPHANT

On land, the African bush elephant is the daddy of all mammals. The largest of these tremendous tuskers busts the scales at 11 t (10 mt)—that's about the same weight as five pickup trucks or 22 cows.

ELEPHANT SEAL

Weighing up to 9,000 lb (4,000 kg), the male southern elephant seal is the largest living carnivore (powerfully jawed, meat-eating mammal). Hunting for squid and fish, southern elephant seals can dive up to 7,000 ft (2,000 m) below the surface, staying submerged for up to two hours at a time.

SUPERSIZE ME!

HOW BIG CAN ANIMALS GET? MAMMALS ARE UNIQUE IN THAT THEY INCLUDE SOME OF THE BIGGEST ANIMALS ON THE PLANET. LET'S MEET FOUR OF THE MOST IMPRESSIVE BEASTS.

BLUE WHALE

The blue whale is the largest known animal ever to have existed. This basketball-court-sized marine mammoth measures 100 ft (30.5 m) from tip to tail and weighs 200 t (180 mt). Its tongue alone weighs about as much as an Asian elephant!

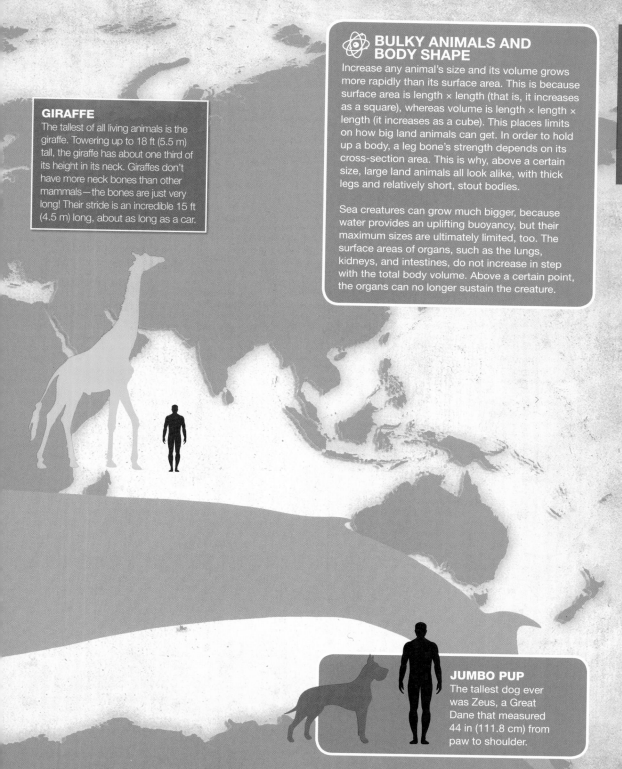

GIRAFFE

The tallest of all living animals is the giraffe. Towering up to 18 ft (5.5 m) tall, the giraffe has about one third of its height in its neck. Giraffes don't have more neck bones than other mammals—the bones are just very long! Their stride is an incredible 15 ft (4.5 m) long, about as long as a car.

BULKY ANIMALS AND BODY SHAPE

Increase any animal's size and its volume grows more rapidly than its surface area. This is because surface area is length × length (that is, it increases as a square), whereas volume is length × length × length (it increases as a cube). This places limits on how big land animals can get. In order to hold up a body, a leg bone's strength depends on its cross-section area. This is why, above a certain size, large land animals all look alike, with thick legs and relatively short, stout bodies.

Sea creatures can grow much bigger, because water provides an uplifting buoyancy, but their maximum sizes are ultimately limited, too. The surface areas of organs, such as the lungs, kidneys, and intestines, do not increase in step with the total body volume. Above a certain point, the organs can no longer sustain the creature.

JUMBO PUP

The tallest dog ever was Zeus, a Great Dane that measured 44 in (111.8 cm) from paw to shoulder.

17

THE WORLD'S OLDEST CREATURES

FROM ANCIENT 11,000-YEAR-OLD SEA SPONGES TO 400-YEAR-OLD CLAMS, SOME ANIMALS LIVE FANTASTICALLY LONG LIVES. THESE ARE PLANET EARTH'S LONGEST-LIVING BEASTS.

WORLD EVENTS

Woolly mammoths become extinct in North America (c. 9000 B.C.E.)

Galileo observes the moons of Jupiter (1610)

Pilgrims land at Plymouth Rock (1620)

USA declares independence (1776)

DATE OF BIRTH

c. 9000 B.C.E.

The oceans are home to the planet's longest-living animals. Scientists discovered an 11,000-year-old sponge deep in the East China Sea.

1600s

Some quahog clams claim a clam-tastic age of 400 years.

1610s

Greenland sharks often get to 200 years old. One individual, however, sharked around for 400 years, making it the world's oldest vertebrate.

1750s

Adwaita, an Aldabra giant tortoise, lived to 255 years old at the Alipore Zoological Gardens in Calcutta, India (c.1750–2006). He was the world's oldest land animal ever.

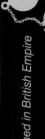

1750s
Most koi fish live for up to 30 years, but one famous Japanese koi called Hanako lived to 226 years.

French Revolution (1789–1799)

Slavery abolished in British Empire (1833)

1800s
Bowhead whales are the world's longest-lived mammal. They live around 200 years on average, and have a whale of a time!

Marie and Pierre Curie discover the first radioactive elements (1898)

1870s
Jeanne Calment lived until she was 122 years and 164 days (1875–1997). Hers is the longest human life ever recorded.

World War I begins (1914)

1910s
Known for their long memories, elephants also live long lives—up to 70 years. Lin Wang (1917–2003), an Asian elephant in Taipei Zoo, reached 86 years old.

The "Star-Spangled Banner" becomes USA's national anthem (1931)

World War II begins (1939)

Francis Crick and James Watson discover the structure of DNA (1953)

First human on the moon (1969)

1960s
Cats may have nine lives, but they rarely live longer than 15 years. Creme Puff from Texas (1967–2005) lived for 38 years.

First cell phone introduced to the public (1983)

1980s
Max (1983–2013) smashed the 13-year average lifespan of most dogs. He made it to 29 years and 282 days. It's a dog's life!

ALL LEGS!

FORGET NOT HAVING A LEG TO STAND ON—THESE CRITTERS HAVE ENOUGH FOR EVERYONE! HERE ARE THE CREEPIEST CREEPY-CRAWLERS ON THE PLANET.

650 LEGS!
MILLIPEDES

A "thousand-legger"? Not quite! The millipede with the most legs is *Illacme plenipes*, with 325 pairs. That's a whopping 650 legs—but still shy of the full 1,000. Most millipedes have less than 200 pairs of legs. Perhaps when millipedes were first named, people couldn't be bothered to count them!

354 LEGS!
CENTIPEDES

The legs champ of the centipede world has 354 legs. The main difference between centipedes and millipedes is that centipedes have two legs per segment, while millipedes have four legs per segment. Centipedes are also deadly predators of bugs, while millipedes are simply mild mulch-munchers.

86 LEGS!
VELVET WORMS

Described as "worms with legs," beautiful velvet worms grow up to 6 in (15 cm) long, and look like a cross between a caterpillar and a slug. These strange land creatures can have as many as 43 pairs of stubby little feet. The velvet worm's secret weapon is a sticky slime, which it shoots out to snare prey.

16 LEGS!
CATERPILLARS

Plump caterpillars are the leggy larvae of moths and butterflies. Many larvae of large moths and butterflies have 16 legs—three pairs of true legs and five pairs of "prolegs" on their bellies. Prolegs act like legs, but they aren't segmented like true legs. When the caterpillar becomes an adult, they are lost.

14 LEGS!
WOOD LICE

Roly-poly pill bugs have plentiful pins. But they have almost as many names. Also known as armadillo bugs, cheesy bobs, doodlebugs, chiggy pigs, granny grays, and butcher boys, wood lice have 14 legs.

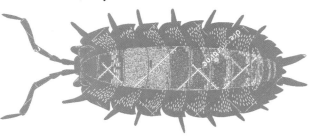

8 LEGS!
SPIDERS

The world's creepiest creepy-crawlers have an unmistakable eight legs, but did you know that spiders also have eight eyes? Weird! The world-record-holding largest spider is Rosi, a Goliath bird-eating tarantula, who weighed in at 6 oz (170 g) and legs that spanned 11 in (28 cm) long! That's as big as a dinner plate!

6 LEGS!
INSECTS

All insects—ants, lice, houseflies, beetles, bees, and butterflies—have six legs. With more than one million different species, insects are the single most successful group of animals. They account for three-quarters of all known animal species.

LEGGY LEGEND
Illacme plenipes means "in highest fulfillment of feet."

THE WORLD'S TOUGHEST CREATURES

LIFE CAN GET ROUGH, BUT THESE LIVING THINGS SEEM TO ENJOY TAKING IT TO THE EXTREME. THESE BRAWNY BEASTS HANG OUT ON THE VERY EDGE AND ENDURE INCREDIBLE HARDSHIPS.

INDESTRUCTIBLE INVERTEBRATES

Although they are smaller than poppy seeds, water bears make other tough creatures look pathetic. When life gets tough, these cute little critters enter a "freeze-dried" survival mode. They can stay in this state for 30 years, but add a little water, and they magically reanimate.

HARDSHIP RECORD	30 years dried out
TROUBLE INDEX	Temperatures near absolute zero (−459.67 °F/−273.15 °C); Frying at 302 °F (150 °C)
SURVIVAL INSTINCT	10 days in space

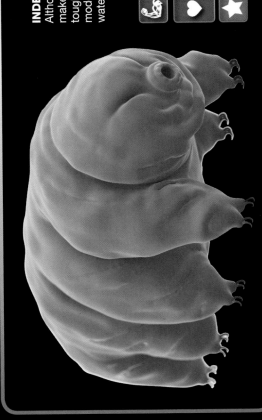

HARD AS SNAILS

As well as holding the record for the largest land snail, the giant African snail is also one of the world's top invasive species. This slimy bigfoot moves across the land, chomping every plant in its path.

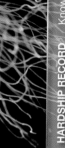

HARDSHIP RECORD Three years of drought

EXTREME JELLY

Turritopsis dohrnii, the immortal jellyfish, goes back to its earliest stage of life—a polyp—when it gets stressed out. It can do this again and again—so long as it doesn't get injured or eaten, this 0.18-in-long (4.5 mm) jelly can live forever!

HARDSHIP RECORD Knows the secret of eternal life

COOL CUSTOMER

Living things are full of water. If it freezes, delicate cells and vessels burst. Antarctic icefish have antifreeze proteins in their blood and large hearts that keep the blood pumping around their bodies in ice-cold waters.

HARDSHIP RECORD Seawater temperatures of 28 °F (−2 °C)

BACTERIAL BULLY

Some single-celled living things bathe in battery-acid hot springs. The meanest microbe is *Deinococcus radiodurans*, "Conan the Bacterium." Blast this invincible bug's DNA apart with a dose of deadly radiation and it repairs itself.

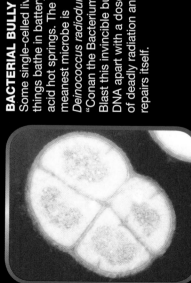

HARDSHIP RECORD 5,000 gray (500,000 rad)—units of ionizing radiation

LONGEST MIGRATIONS

SOME ANIMALS UNDERTAKE EPIC JOURNEYS. EVERY YEAR, THESE CHAMPION TRAVELERS SET OFF TO SPEND THE SUMMER WHERE THE WEATHER IS BETTER, THE FOOD MORE PLENTIFUL, AND THERE ARE MORE OPPORTUNITIES TO MEET A PARTNER.

SERENGETI MIGRATION
(wildebeest, zebra, gazelle, eland, impala)

Distance: 500 miles (800 km)
Journey: Circular migration around the Ngorongoro Conservation Area of the southern Serengeti, Tanzania

MONARCH BUTTERFLIES

Distance: 3,000 miles (4,800 km)
Journey: North America to the southern part of California and Mexico. It takes three to four generations of butterflies to make the return journey.

Distance in miles

| 1,000 | 2,000 | 3,000 | 4,000 | 5,000 | 6,000 |

CARIBOU

Distance: 3,100 miles (5,000 km)
Journey: Large herds of up to 500,000 caribou move south from northern Arctic regions.

SALMON

Distance: 6,000 miles (9,700 km)
Journey: After two to three years in the sea, salmon return to the river where they were born to breed.

DRAGONFLIES

Distance: 10,000 miles (16,000 km)
Journey: South Asia to Africa, taking about four generations to complete a full migration

ANIMAL PATHFINDERS

Many animals have an amazing ability to travel thousands and thousands of miles and find their way to the same spot every year. How do they do it?

GENETICS

Some scientists believe parents may pass migratory routes to their offspring in their genes.

COMMUNICATION

Animals that migrate in groups call and signal between each other to help them navigate and stick together.

MENTAL MAPS

Remembering landmarks on a route may help with simple migrations. Gray whales follow ups and downs of the ocean floor, for example.

MAGNETIC FIELD

Some animals have the ability to detect Earth's magnetic field. Homing pigeons and dolphins are thought to use it to navigate.

SUN AND MOON

Many birds and insects get their bearings by tracking the path of the sun or moon.

STARS

Like ancient mariners, mallard ducks find north using bright stars in the sky.

SMELL

Salmon use scent to spawn in the exact same place where they were hatched themselves. Scientists believe that wildebeest can smell rain to get to green pastures.

OCEAN CURRENTS

Some fish deliberately swim against ocean currents to find their way to breeding grounds.

LEATHERBACK SEA TURTLES

Distance: Often more than 10,000 miles (16,000 km)
Journey: Across the Atlantic and Pacific Oceans

SOOTY SHEARWATER

Distance: 40,000 miles (64,000 km)
Journey: New Zealand to North Pacific Ocean

Distance in miles

| 10,000 | 15,000 | 20,000 | 25,000 | 30,000 | 35,000 | 40,000 | 45,000 |

NORTHERN ELEPHANT SEALS

Distance: 13,000 miles (21,000 km)
Journey: Coast of California to Alaska and back

HUMPBACK WHALES

Distance: Up to 11,700 miles (18,800 km)
Journey: Tropical to polar waters

ARCTIC TERN

Distance: 44,000 miles (71,000 km)
Journey: Between Greenland and Antarctica

MY NEST IS BIGGER THAN YOURS!

WHEN IT COMES TO BUILDING NESTS, MANY BIRDS ARE JUDGED BY THEIR CONSTRUCTION SKILLS, SO IT HELPS TO THINK BIG. BUT WHO HAS THE BEST NEST?

DIMENSIONS

 9 ft 6 in (2.9 m)
20 ft (6 m)

 4,409 lb (2 mt)

WORLD RECORD BREAKER!
BALD AMBITION
A bald eagle's house is so grand, it's not even called a nest. This country pile (of twigs

DIMENSIONS

 20 × 13 ft (6 × 4 m)
7 ft (2.1 m)

2,000 lb (900 kg)

MEGA NEST!

The most ginormous nests belong to the sociable weaver. These "mega nests" reach sizes of 20 × 13 × 7 ft (6 × 4 × 2 m) and can weigh more than 2,000 lb (900 kg). They house hundreds of breeding pairs. They are so well constructed, they can last over a century —that is, if they don't collapse the trees they're built in!

FAIRY CUPS

The ruby-throated hummingbird makes a fairy-tale house from bud scales and leaf strands bound together with spider silk. The thimble-sized nest is delicately decorated with lichen and lined with thistledown—just perfect for three tiny, less than ⅟₅₀ oz (½ gram) eggs.

DIMENSIONS

 1 in (2.5 cm)
2 in (5 cm)

HUMAN BODY RECORD BREAKER

HUMANS ARE INCREDIBLE, AND THEIR BODIES COME IN ALL SHAPES AND SIZES. PREPARE TO BE AMAZED AND INSPIRED (AND A LITTLE GROSSED OUT) BY THESE RECORD-BREAKING BODIES THAT DEFY BELIEF!

RAPUNZEL, RAPUNZEL!

The longest hair in the world belongs to Xie Qiuping of China. Combed out and measured in 2004, it stretched 18 ft 5.54 in (5.627 m) long—that's about as long as a giraffe is tall!

ALL FINGERS AND THUMBS

The living person with the most fingers and toes is Devendra Suthar of India. He has a grand total of 28—that's a quick-counting 14 fingers and 14 toes.

POPEYE

Kim Goodman of the USA has the startling ability to pop her eyeballs 0.47 in (12 mm) out of their sockets. Yikes!

BIGNOSE

The longest nose on the planet is a tremendous 3.46 in (8.8 cm) from bridge to the tip. Mehmet Özyürek of Turkey is the proud owner of this prize snout.

3.46 in
(8.8 cm)

TUFTY-EARS

Victor Anthony from India sports the world's hairiest ears. The tufts growing from his ears are a tickly 7.12 in (18.1 cm) long.

SCRATCH THAT ITCH!

Shridhar Chillal of India stopped cutting the fingernails on his left hand in 1952. As of 2015, the total length of those fingernails is a curly-wurly 358.1 in (909.6 cm). His thumbnail is the longest at 77.87 in (197.8 cm).

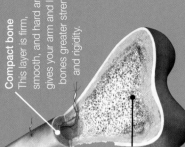

BOUNCING BONES

Your bones protect your vital organs, provide a framework on which to hang your organs, and attach to muscles to move around. They are constructed in four layers.

Periosteum (say perry-OSS-tee-um)
This thin outer covering carries nerves and blood vessels to sustain your bone.

Compact bone
This layer is firm, smooth, and hard and gives your arm and leg bones greater strength and rigidity.

Marrow
The insides of the bigger bones in your body are filled with a thick jelly called bone marrow. Red blood cells are made in the marrow and pumped out into your body.

Spongy bone
Within the compact are layers of spongy bone. While not as hard as compact bone, spongy bone is still very strong.

HIGH AND MIGHTY

The tallest human being living on the planet is Sultan Kösen of Turkey. Measuring a mighty 8 ft, 2.8 in (2.51 m) tall, he's certainly no wallflower. Robert Wadlow (USA), who died in 1940, was even loftier, measuring a full 8 ft, 11.1 in (2.72 m) tall.

8 ft, 2.8 in (2.51 m)

26.41 in (67.08 cm)

TINY TOTS

The shortest person alive today is Khagendra Thapa Magar. Born in 1992, this Nepalese prizewinner measures just 2 ft 2.41 in (67.08 cm) tall.

BIGFOOT

The biggest feet in the world belong to a 7-foot-tall Venezuelan teenager. Jeison Orlando Rodríguez Hernández's right foot measures a mighty 15.8 in (40.1 cm).

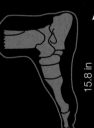

15.8 in (40.1 cm)

3000 B.C.E.–1500 B.C.E.
Stonehenge
Salisbury Plain,
UK **30 ft** (9 m)
Built using earthworks,
wooden frames,
and levers.

2500 B.C.E.
Great Pyramid
Giza, Egypt
481.4 ft (147 m) when built
World's tallest structure for
3,800 years; erosion has
made it shorter.

c.2500 B.C.E.
4.4-t (4 mt) stones transported 140
miles (225 km) on rollers and sleds

c.2500 B.C.E.
20–25,000 slaves shift more than two million
blocks of 2.5–6 t (2.3 –5.4 mt) rock up ramps

1889
Eiffel Tower
Paris, France
1,063 ft (324 m), inc. antenna
World's tallest structure from
1889 to 1929. Framework
uses 8,050 t (7,300 mt) of
wrought iron.

1885
Home Insurance Building
Chicago, USA
138 ft (42 m)
The world's first skyscraper.
An internal cage of iron beams
bears the weight instead of
outer walls.

1851
Crystal Palace
London, UK
128 ft (39 m)
The greatest area of glass
ever seen. Supported by
1,000 iron columns.

1931
Empire State Building
New York City, USA
1,250 ft (381 m)
World's tallest building
from 1931 to 1972.
First use of "fast-track
construction," where
building begins before
designs are finished.

1930s
Invention of
insulated glass

1913
Woolworth Building
New York City, USA
792 ft (241.4 m)
The "Cathedral of Commerce"
was the world's tallest building
from 1913 to 1930.

⚛ AS STRONG AS CONCRETE

When things are built with concrete,
they are made to last. Concrete
actually gains strength over time.
It starts off as a wet mixture of
cement, sand, water, and crushed
rock. Chemical reactions then
make it hard. Reinforced concrete
combines concrete and steel. They
make a dream team: Concrete is
strong when squeezed, but weak
when stretched; steel is flexible
and strong when stretched. Setting
steel bars or cables into concrete
when it is poured combines the best
properties of both materials.

c.128 c.e.
Pantheon
Rome, Italy
142 ft (43.3 m) in diameter
The world's largest
unreinforced concrete
dome to this day.

1311
Lincoln Cathedral
Lincoln, UK
525 ft (160 m), when completed
World's tallest building, until a storm
in 1548. High walls supported by
flying buttresses.

c.2000 b.c.e.
Romans develop a hard-wearing
concrete mortar

c.1120
Pointed arches and rib vaults
allow larger, taller churches

BUILD 'EM HIGH

**INNOVATIONS AND ADVANCES IN MATERIALS
AND TECHNOLOGY HAVE ALLOWED PEOPLE
TO BUILD TALLER AND TALLER BUILDINGS.
HERE'S A BRIEF HISTORY OF OUR RACE TO
SCRAPE THE SKIES.**

1850s
First reinforced
concrete

1850s
First industrially
produced steel

c.1500
Invention of
the pile driver

1974
Sears Tower
(now Willis Tower)
Chicago, USA
1,450 ft (442 m)
World's tallest building
from 1973 to 1996. Built
as a "bundled tube" of
nine square cylinders.

2010
Burj Khalifa
Dubai, United Arab Emirates
2,716.5 ft (828 m)
The world's tallest building. The
steel used for the tower would
stretch one-quarter of the way
around the planet.

1949
Invention of the
tower crane

DID YOU KNOW?
The Burj Khalifa is
so tall, the outside
temperature can be
15 °F (9 °C) cooler at
the top of the building
than it is at the base.

Blue Whale
The largest animal on Earth measures just 100 ft (30 m) head to tail.

Empire State Building

MV *Barzan* container ship

MEGA SHIP!

MV *BARZAN* IS ONE OF SEVERAL SHIPS THAT MEASURE 1,300 FT (400 M) LONG. THESE VESSELS ARE THE WORLD'S LONGEST SHIPS. THEY ARE AS LONG AS FOUR SOCCER FIELDS—A DISTANCE THAT MATCHES THE HEIGHT OF NEW YORK'S EMPIRE STATE BUILDING!

MV *Barzan* is named for historical fortified watchtowers that look out to sea in Qatar.

INSTAFACTS

MV Barzan

Owned by: United Arab Shipping Company (UASC)

Year built: 2015

Length: 1312 ft (400 m)

Width: 192 ft (58.6 m)

The supertanker *Knock Nevis* was the largest ship ever built. The 1,500-ft-long (458 m) monster ship was scrapped in 2010.

33

TO THE MAX

MAX

CHAPTER 2

DID YOU KNOW?

A great white shark has several rows of super-sharp serrated teeth—up to 300 in total. Yet with a force that measures around 2,000 PSI (pounds per square inch; 141 kg/cm²), this toothy terror has barely more bite than a hungry hippo (see page **45**).

STARLIGHT EXPRESS

SUPER-FAST OBJECTS RULE, AND THERE'S NO BETTER PLACE FOR THEM THAN IN SPACE—A ZONE OF ASTRONOMICAL NUMBERS AND MIND-BLOWING DIMENSIONS.

SUN
Our star orbits the Milky Way's center at an eye-watering 514,000 MPH (828,000 kmh). The galaxy is so big, it takes the sun 230 million years to complete one huge loop.

MERCURY
The speediest planet in the solar system is Mercury. As the closest planet to the sun, it travels 36 million miles (60,000 km) in a year. The planet travels at 106,000 MPH (171,000 kmh) and takes 88 days to circle the sun.

Mercury travels 48 times faster than a MiG-25, the fastest fighter jet in the world.

EARTH
Strap yourself in. You are currently hurtling through space at about 67,000 MPH (108,000 kmh). That's 100 times faster than a passenger airplane. Earth takes 365.25 days to make the 584-million-mile (940 million km) trip around the sun.

IN A WHIRL
Earth measures 25,000 miles (40,000 km) around its equator and turns on its own axis once every 23 hours, 56 minutes, and 4 seconds. This means we are spinning at roughly 1,000 MPH (1,600 kmh). Feeling dizzy?

HYPERVELOCITY STAR

In 2005, scientists discovered a super-fast star streaking across the cosmos. The star, with the catchy name SDSS J090745.0+024507, was spotted leaving the galaxy at 1.9 million MPH (3 million kmh).

COSMIC CANNONBALL

RX J0822-4300 is a neutron star traveling at more than 3 million MPH (4.8 million kmh)—nearly six times faster than our sun. It was blasted into space during an explosion that ended the life of its parent star.

BLOBS IN BLAZARS

The speed demons of the universe are blobs of super-hot gas shot out from mega-high-energy galaxies called blazars. Embedded in jets of material streaming into space, they travel at an incredible 99.9 percent of the speed of light.

THE SPEED OF LIGHT

Things in space certainly know how to get a move on, but the highways of the universe do have speed limits. The laws of physics mean that nothing can travel faster than the speed of light. This ultimate speed is 671 million MPH (1,079 million kmh).

GLACIERS

GLACIERS ARE GREAT EXPANSES OF ICE THAT MOVE VERY SLOWLY. THEY CHANGE THE WORLD BY SCULPTING PEAKS, WEARING DOWN MIGHTY MOUNTAINS, AND CARVING OUT VAST VALLEYS.

SNOW + TIME = GLACIER

Glaciers form where snow builds up on mountainsides and doesn't melt over summer. As snow falls upon snow, it compresses to form solid ice. Once ice gets to around 66 ft (20 m) thick, it begins to move downhill when pressure caused by its weight starts melting its bottom layer.

 Glaciers are like really slow rivers. They flow downhill at snail speeds of about 10 in (25 cm) a day.

 Ice crystals in glaciers can grow to the size of a baseball. *Brrr!*

 Glacial ice is so compacted, it often looks bright blue in color!

 Glacier speed record: 150 ft (46 m) per day (Jakobshavn Glacier in Greenland).

 GLACIAL GRINDSTONE

Glaciers tear up terrain in a process called "plucking." Melted water flows into cracks in the bedrock and refreezes, splintering the rock apart. Entire chunks of rock are swallowed up into the ice. As a glacier slides over the ground, the pressure of tons of compressed snow grinds down bedrock, producing superfine "rock flour." Over time, glaciers carve out wide, U-shaped valleys.

DID YOU KNOW?

Glaciers can last a very long time—from a few hundred years to hundreds of thousands of years. Ice cores taken from glaciers sometimes contain bubbles of trapped air from the ancient atmosphere. Ice cores help scientists learn about what the climate was like on Earth thousands of years ago.

BIG DRIP

Global warming is causing glaciers to melt on all continents. This—along with melting ice caps and sea ice, and ocean water expanding in volume—is causing Earth's sea levels to rise.

 Giant cracks called crevasses open on the surface of a moving glacier. They can be as deep as 150 ft (46 m).

 Antarctica's Lambert Glacier is the largest glacier on Earth. It spans 60 miles (96 km) across, stretches about 270 miles (435 km) long, and is 1.6 miles (2.5 km) deep in places.

 About three-quarters of the world's freshwater is locked up inside glaciers.

Australia is the only large landmass on Earth without glaciers.

ANIMAL POWER

WELCOME TO THE ULTIMATE COMPETITION TO FIND THE WORLD'S STRONGEST ANIMAL. NATURE'S HEAVYWEIGHTS (AND LIGHTWEIGHTS) GO HEAD-TO-HEAD TO BE CROWNED KING OF THE BEASTS! FIND OUT IF IT'S BETTER TO BE BIG AND BEEFY, OR SMALL AND STRONG.

BIG BLUE BOSS

A blue whale mom has no trouble carrying a 6,000-lb (2,700 kg) baby! But it's easier to lift things in water because of the upward force of buoyancy it provides.

Body weight: 331,000 lb (150,000 kg)
Pulling power: more than 13,000 lb (6,000 kg)
Relative strength: x0.04

TERRIFIC TUSKER

Working in teams, Asian elephants can move 3.5–4.5 t (3–4 mt) of logs a day. A single Asian elephant is thought to be able to lift 660 lb (300 kg) with its trunk.

Body weight: 12,000 lb (5,400 kg)
Pulling power: 19,800 lb (9,000 kg)
Relative strength: x1.67

HORSEPOWER

Draft horses are large, strong-legged horses bred for heavy work. In the time of the Crusades, Percheron horses were used as warhorses. Later, they became America's favorite horse for heavy farm work. A draft horse can easily pull twice its weight.

Body weight: 2,600 lb (1,180 kg)
Pulling power: 4,400 lb (2,000 kg)
Relative strength: x1.69

BIGGER ANIMALS CAN LIFT LARGER WEIGHTS, BUT INSECTS ARE THE REAL BEASTS OF BURDEN. WHEN COMPARED TO THEIR BODY WEIGHTS, THESE TINY TOTS ARE WAY STRONGER THAN YOU MIGHT THINK!

AWESOME ANT

In 2010, an Asian weaver ant was photographed lifting 100 times its own body weight. Ants use the stickiness of their feet to help them lift weights, and can even change the size of their foot pads.

Relative strength: x100

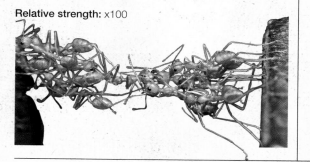

BODYBUILDING BEETLE

A rhinoceros beetle can move 100 times its body weight. That's a good thing, because this critter spends much of its time burrowing through the rotting wood of fallen logs.

Relative strength: x100

WORLD CHAMP

When it comes to feats of strength, dung beetles are top of the heap. The horned dung beetle can deadlift 1,141 times its own body weight. That's like a human lifting six 43-ft-long (13 m) buses!

Relative strength: x1,141

FASTEST ANIMALS

IN NATURE, A BURST OF SPEED CAN MAKE THE DIFFERENCE BETWEEN CATCHING A MEAL AND AVOIDING BECOMING SOME OTHER ANIMAL'S DINNER. THESE SPEED FREAKS OF THE ANIMAL KINGDOM LEAVE US HUMANS GASPING FOR BREATH.

SPECIAL MENTION

Although it wouldn't beat many beasts in a foot race, the South California mite is the fastest animal on the planet relative to the length of its body. This mighty mite speeds along at 322 body lengths per second—a human being running this fast would be doing 1,300 MPH (2,100 kmh)!

PEREGRINE FALCON
200 MPH (320 kmh)
This daredevil bird of prey takes the title of world's fastest animal, thanks to its heart-stopping hunting dive at speeds of 200 MPH (320 kmh).

WHITE-THROATED NEEDLETAIL SWIFT
105 MPH (169 kmh)
Believed to be the world's fastest level-flying bird, the needletail swift's speed comes from powered flapping flight.

EURASIAN HOBBY
99 MPH (159 kmh)
These powerfully fast flappers sometimes outgun swifts. A hobby is a type of falcon. Its speed and flying skills allow it to snatch swallows and swifts out of the air.

42

OSTRICH
43 MPH (69 kmh)
As well as laying the largest eggs on Earth, this whiz leaves other flightless birds in its dust. Sprinting across the African savanna, the ostrich is the fastest bird on land.

PRONGHORN ANTELOPE
53 MPH (85 kmh)
This North American native has top speeds of around 53 MPH (85 kmh). When migrating, it can run at half that speed for 250 miles (400 km) and more.

CHEETAH
61 MPH (98 kmh)
The undisputed champ of the short sprint, the cheetah has incredible acceleration. This African all-star goes from 0 to 60 MPH (0 to 100 kmh) in just three seconds.

SAILFISH
68 MPH (110 kmh)
The fabulous flying sailfish reaches speeds of 68 MPH (110 kmh) when leaping out of the water. This fish has a magnificent sail-like dorsal fin.

BLACK MARLIN
80 MPH (129 kmh)
Known for its long, pointed bill, the black marlin is found in the Indian and Pacific Oceans. It has been recorded unwinding fishing line at 80 MPH (129 kmh).

SWORDFISH
81 MPH (130 kmh)
Studies suggest that the swordfish can use its streamlined body, sharp bill, and curved tail fin to propel itself forward at a maximum speed of 81 MPH (130 kmh).

BITE

MEET THE MIGHTY MUNCHERS AND CRUSHING CRUNCHERS WITH THE SCARIEST JAWS ON EARTH. SCIENTISTS HAVE ONLY RECENTLY STARTED TO INVESTIGATE BITE FORCE. THEY DO THIS BY MEASURING HOW MANY POUNDS OF FORCE AN ANIMAL APPLIES PER SQUARE INCH (PSI FOR SHORT). WHICH ANIMAL HAS THE STRONGEST BITE OF ALL?

Megalodon's serrated teeth could grow to over 7 in (17 cm) long.

40,000 PSI

BIGGEST BITE . . . EVER!
Megalodon was a giant shark, known as "Big Tooth." This 50-ft (16 m) prehistoric monster had the most powerful bite ever: up to 40,000-PSI (2,810 kg/cm²).

DID YOU KNOW?

Enormous jaw-closing muscles give crocodiles their fearsome bites.

3,700 PSI

MAKE IT SNAPPY
The top three biters in the world are all crocodilians. The biggest, the saltwater crocodile, slams its jaws shut with a record-breaking 3,700 PSI (260 kg/cm²).

200 PSI

TINY TERROR
Most hard biters are big animals, but it's not all about size. Pound for pound, the overall champ is the Tasmanian devil, with a mighty bite force compared to its small body mass. This 26-lb (12 kg) marsupial muncher bites down with 200 PSI (14 kg/cm^2).

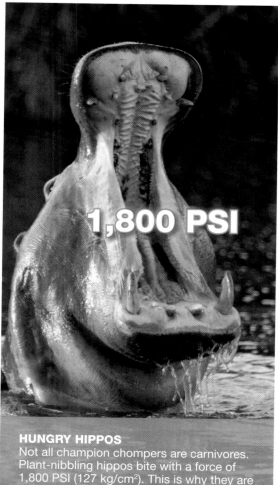

1,800 PSI

1,500 PSI

HUNGRY HIPPOS
Not all champion chompers are carnivores. Plant-nibbling hippos bite with a force of 1,800 PSI (127 kg/cm^2). This is why they are one of the most feared animals in Africa.

COOL FOR CATS
A jaguar is the wildcat with the biggest bite. This South American big cat can generate 1,500 PSI (105 kg/cm^2), allowing it to tear into a turtle shell.

ANIMALS IN SPACE

ASTRONAUTS HAVE MADE QUITE A FEW FIRSTS IN SPACE, BUT THE TRUE SPACE PIONEERS ARE PUPS, FLIES, FISH, MICE, MONKEYS, AND MOTHS! ASTRONAUTS HAVE ALWAYS GONE BOLDLY WHERE ANIMALS HAVE GONE BEFORE.

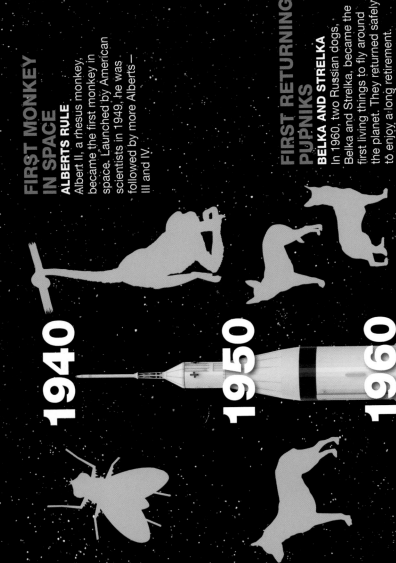

1940

1950

1960

FIRST ANIMAL IN SPACE
FRUIT FLIES

After World War II, fruit flies flew in the nose cone of a captured German V-2 rocket. American scientists made the launch in 1947, to test the effects of radiation on living things.

FIRST ANIMAL TO ORBIT EARTH
LAIKA

In 1957, the Russian "muttnik" Laika made the journey into space and looped the planet aboard *Sputnik 2*. Before she was selected for the flight, she was called Kudryavka, meaning *Little Curly*.

FIRST MONKEY IN SPACE
ALBERTS RULE

Albert II, a rhesus monkey, became the first monkey in space. Launched by American scientists in 1949, he was followed by more Alberts— III and IV.

FIRST RETURNING PUPNIKS
BELKA AND STRELKA

In 1960, two Russian dogs, Belka and Strelka, became the first living things to fly around the planet. They returned safely to enjoy a long retirement.

FIRST CREATURES TO THE MOON

NOAH'S SPACE ARK

In 1968, the Russian lunar probe *Zond 5* set off for the moon with a cargo of turtles, wine flies, mealworms, plants, seeds, and bacteria. These were the first living things to fly to the moon. The pilot was said to be a 5-ft 9-in, (175 cm), 154-lb (70 kg) mannequin!

FIRST ORBITING CHIMP

ENOS

The first American to orbit Earth was Enos the chimp. In 1961, he rode a Mercury Atlas 5 rocket twice around the planet before returning to Earth.

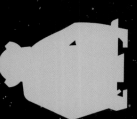

FIRST SPIDERWEB IN SPACE

WEB-BUILDING EXPERIMENT

Two spiders, Anita and Arabella, stayed on *Skylab 3*, the US–Russian space station, in 1973, in an experiment designed to look at the effects of microgravity on the spiders' ability to build webs. After a shaky start, the pair were soon spinning wonderful webs.

1970

WHY PUT ANIMALS INTO SPACE?

The first animals were sent into space to check that the environment was safe enough for humans. No one knew what the effects of space flight, microgravity, and intense radiation would be. Could astronauts suffocate on their food as it floated free in their stomachs, for example? No one knew. There is no question that many of the early experiments were cruel. Many animals were very stressed and some even died in space.

FIRST ANIMALS TO SURVIVE A SPACE ACCIDENT

WRIGGLE ANOTHER DAY

When the space shuttle *Columbia* broke up on re-entry in 2003, all seven astronauts on board tragically lost their lives. However, against all logic and likelihood, worms were recovered from the wreckage, still alive.

2000

47

ACCELERATION!

SPEED DEMONS OF THE WORLD UNITE! THESE HOT RODS ARE HEADING FOR HIGH-SPEED HEAVEN, SO LET'S FIND OUT WHICH VEHICLE IS FASTEST OFF THE BLOCKS.

FASTEST PRODUCTION MOTORCYCLE

0 to 60 MPH
2.35 seconds

GREASED LIGHTNING

Reaching 0 to 60 MPH (0 to 100 kmh) in just 2.35 seconds, the Suzuki GSX-R1000 is not a custom motorcycle or a specialized racing bike, but rolls off the production lines ready to rock!

FASTEST PRODUCTION CAR

0 to 60 MPH
2.2 seconds

RAPID ROADSTER

The speediest acceleration from a standing start to 60 MPH (0–100 kmh) is 2.2 seconds in a Porsche 918 Spyder.

FASTEST TRAIN

373 MPH

WORLD'S FASTEST ACCELERATING VEHICLE

0 to 100 MPH
less than a second

FASTER THAN A SPEEDING BULLET

Floating on frictionless magnets, Japan's cutting-edge L0 series maglev train can cover 1.1 miles (1.8 km) in 11 seconds. In 2015, the train set a world-record speed of 373 MPH (600 kmh).

WHAT A DRAG!

Top Fuel dragsters accelerate from a standing start to 100 MPH (160 kmh) in less than a hair-raising second!

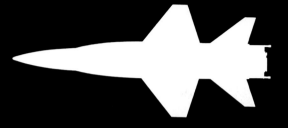

SWIFTEST AIRCRAFT
7,310 MPH

HYPERSONIC STREAKER
NASA's experimental rocket plane, the *X-43 A*, is the fastest aircraft ever made. Its top speed is 7,310 MPH (11,760 kmh)—that's more than nine times faster than the speed of sound!

SPEEDIEST MANNED VEHICLE
24,791 MPH

SPACE TRAVEL
Launched in 1969, *Apollo 10* was the "dress rehearsal" for America's moon landing. The command module, nicknamed Charlie Brown, topped 24,791 MPH (39,897 kmh) on its way back from the moon—the highest speed yet achieved by a manned vehicle.

FASTEST HUMAN-MADE OBJECT
221,232 MPH

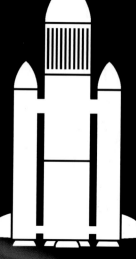

HELIOS 2
NASA's *Helios 2* space probe holds the record for the fleetest object ever made by humankind. As the sun-grazing spacecraft sped away from Earth in 1989, it hit 221,232 MPH (356,038 kmh).

 SPEED VS. ACCELERATION
You want to go faster? You'll have to accelerate. *Acceleration* means change of speed. An object can be moving extremely fast and still not be accelerating. The faster speed increases, the greater the acceleration. Vehicles traveling through space have small accelerations, but over great distances they can reach enormous speeds.

49

FASTEST MAN ON EARTH

WHEN THE "LIGHTNING BOLT" EXPLODES FROM THE STARTING BLOCKS, THERE'S NO STOPPING HIM.

Usain St. Leo Bolt is simply the fastest person who has ever lived on the planet. No human past or present could beat him in a footrace over 100 meters and 200 meters. Measuring 6 ft 5 in (195 cm) tall, the Jamaican runner is built for speed, but he also gets extra help from some high-tech equipment.

IT'S IN THE GENES
Scientific studies show that champion racers have a "sprinting gene," which boosts the fast-twitch fibers in their muscles.

SLINKY GEAR
Stretchy fabric with drag-reducing "dimples" allows sprinters to shave milliseconds off their time.

WORLD'S FASTEST PERSON
Usain Bolt holds world records in 100-meter and 200-meter races, and also as a part of the 4x100-meter men's relay team. He is the first person to have won gold medals in both 100-meter and 200-meter events at three Olympics in a row.

World record (100 meters): 9.58 s (2009)
World record (200 meters): 19.19 s (2009)

LARGE HEART
The sprinter's heart may be larger than average and pumps a faster flow of oxygen to his hard-working muscles.

LONG LEGS

The Jamaican giant's stride is about 8 in (20 cm) longer than those of his closest rivals. Bolt takes about 41 steps over 100 m — compared with 43–50 steps of other Olympic sprinters.

SMART SNEAKERS

GPS microchips in sneaker soles track speed, distance, and running patterns. Location info is updated 25 times a second. This helps runners identify the weakest part of their races and train to improve it.

FAST FOOD

At the 2008 Beijing Olympics, Usain "bolted" about 100 chicken nuggets a day. Chicken is a great source of protein, which helps with muscle repair, but it is better eaten lean!

BIOMECHANICS

The greatest sprinter of all time has longer-than-average muscle fiber bundles in his legs, while the tendons in his ankles are relatively short, allowing his muscles to work at high speeds.

CONTACT TIME

At top speed, an elite sprinter spends as much time in the air as on the ground. Each step makes contact with the ground for as little as 0.1 seconds, so it's all about generating as much power as possible in that time.

DID YOU KNOW?

At full speed, Usain Bolt takes a mighty 2.5-m (8.2 ft) step. In the 2008 100-meter Olympic final, he accidentally ran with one shoelace untied . . . and still clocked a world record!

SUPER SENSES

CHAPTER 3

DID YOU KNOW?

A flattened, rubbery bill helps this critter detect the electric field of prey when hunting in murky rivers. But who does this bill belong to? A duck? A mole? Turn to page **61** to find out!

SUPER SMELLS
During the winter months, wolverines are able to sniff out the frozen carcasses of animals trapped deep beneath the snow after an avalanche.

FORKED TONGUE
A snake's tongue picks up on scents as well as taste. The reptile flicks out its tongue, transferring chemicals in the air to a specialized organ that helps pinpoint the source of the smell.

SCENTS OF DANGER
Rats and certain moles can detect a smell "in stereo." This means that each nostril acts separately, allowing the animal to pinpoint more clearly the direction from which a smell is coming—left or right.

MOTH MYTH-TERY
Moths don't bother with a nose. Instead, they hang their scent detectors off their antennae. A male silkworm moth can pick up the odor of a female 1 mile (1.6 km) away.

SMELLS FISHY!
Sharks can detect blood at one part per million— about the same concentration as a teaspoon of blood in an average swimming pool.

SMELL IT

ANIMALS USE THEIR SENSE OF SMELL TO DETECT CHEMICALS IN THE ENVIRONMENT AROUND THEM. HERE ARE SOME ANIMALS WITH THE STRONGEST AND STRANGEST SMELLING ABILITIES.

BEARY GOOD
Black bears can smell prey 18 miles (29 km) away, while polar bears have been known to follow seals for up to 40 miles (64 km).

MASTER TRACKERS
A dog's sense of smell is more than 10,000 times better than our own. With around 300 million scent receptors in their noses (compared to our 6 million), they make terrific trackers.

Bloodhounds can follow a two-day-old trail through busy streets and parks.

⚛ EAU DE TOILET
The skunk uses its stink as a weapon. These black-and-white-striped critters produce a pungent liquid out of their bottoms. Sprayed up to 10 ft (3 m), the skunk's vile brew is nearly impossible to wash off. It can be smelled up to a mile (1.6 km) away and it can even cause temporary blindness!

EARS LOOKING AT YOU

Some owls, like the barn owl, have ears placed at different levels on their heads in order to precisely pinpoint prey. The owl's round face filters out other sounds, allowing it to focus all of its attention on the rustle of small animals in the grass.

Up to 12 kHz

STORM WARNING

An elephant's broad, flat ears make it more receptive to lower frequencies. It can hear thunder up to 310 miles (500 km) away.

Up to 12 kHz

SUPER HEARING

WHAT DOES IT TAKE TO BE A GOOD LISTENER? SOME ANIMALS ARE INCREDIBLY GOOD AT PICKING UP ON VIBRATIONS IN THE AIR AND WATER. THE FREQUENCY OF SOUND WAVES IS MEASURED IN HERTZ (Hz).

Up to 105 kHz

Sound waves travel 4.5 times faster in water than they do in air.

BOTTLE ROCKET

Dolphins use high-pitched clicks to navigate murky waters, locate prey, and communicate with one another. They pick up echoing sounds with their lower jawbones, which pipe vibrations directly to their middle ears. This is known as echolocation.

CATS VS. DOGS

Dogs may have the edge when it comes to smelling, but cats take the crown for hearing. Cat's ears are each outfitted with 32 muscles. The muscles can swivel the ear through 180 degrees, allowing kitties to target the source of a sound with deadly precision!

Up to 45 kHz

Up to 64 kHz

HEARING IN HUMANS

Vibrating waves of air enter the ear canal through the trumpet-shaped outer ear—the pinna. Pressure variations set the eardrum vibrating and three tiny bones—the hammer, anvil, and stirrup—carry these wobbles through the middle ear. The vibrations pass into a fluid-filled spiral called the cochlea. Hairs in the cochlea sense the movement of fluid caused by the sound waves and pass the information to the brain, where the signals are interpreted as sound. Humans hear sounds with frequencies up to 20 kHz.

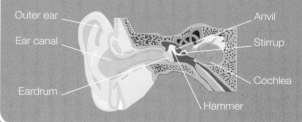

Outer ear
Ear canal
Eardrum
Anvil
Stirrup
Cochlea
Hammer

100 kHz–300kHz

ULTRA EARS

The animal that can detect the highest frequencies is the greater wax moth. This hearing champion's ultrasensitive ears keep it safe from bats.

Up to 110 kHz

SEEING IN SOUND

Bats have terrible night vision! To fly in the pitch dark, they produce high-frequency, ultrasonic squeaks. These sounds reflect really well off surfaces, allowing the bat to "see" the world through sound, hunt down prey while flying, and avoid collisions with objects.

Up to 300 kHz

ANIMAL DECIBELS

MEMBERS OF THE ANIMAL KINGDOM CANNOT BE ACCUSED OF BEING SHY. IT'S A WILD RIOT OF WHOOPS, WHISTLES, AND SCREAMS OUT THERE!

230 dB

200 dB

188 dB

140 dB

120 dB

SPERM WHALE

Chattering sperm whales communicate with clicks that last just one ten-thousandth of a second, but are as loud as 1 t (0.9 MT) of TNT exploding.

TIGER PISTOL SHRIMP

This sharpshooting snapper closes its claws so quickly, they make a deadly sonic weapon. The shockwave caused by the bang kills the shrimp's prey on the spot.

BLUE WHALE

Alone in the ocean, traveling blue whales whistle a happy tune. Louder than an airplane taking off, their calls can be heard over 500 miles (800 km) away.

GREATER BULLDOG BAT

The screeches of these winged night fishermen are as loud as gunshots. Luckily, their ultrasonic screams are way too high-pitched for humans to hear.

GREENGROCER CICADA

These outlandish outback insects beat their hollow tummies like drums. Their chirping can be heard 1.5 miles (2.4 km) away!

117 dB

ELEPHANT

Elephants' rumbling bellows may be too low for the human ear, but elephants 6 miles (10 km) away have no problem picking them up.

115 dB

LION

A male lion stakes out its territory with a terrifying roar lasting over a minute. Everything within a distance of 5 miles (8 km) knows about it!

110 dB

KATYDID

One species of katydid chirps as loudly as a buzz saw buzzes! The male katydid rubs its wings together to attract the attention of far-off females.

100 dB

COQUÍ FROG

Puerto Rico's noisiest inhabitant never stops its incessant chirping. These rowdy rain-forest dwellers make more noise than construction trucks.

100 dB

THREE-WATTLED BELLBIRD

The male three-wattled bellbird has a call that begins with a high-pitched whistle and ends with a loud "bonk" that can be heard up to 0.6 miles (1 km) away.

90 dB

HOWLER MONKEY

The whoops of a howler monkey are as loud as a subway train. Its call is described as a cross between a dog bark and a donkey bray!

WEIRD ANIMAL SENSES

WHAT STRANGE SUPERPOWERS WOULD YOU LIKE TO HAVE? TAKE YOUR PICK FROM THE ANIMAL WORLD. HERE ARE SOME OF THE WACKIEST.

SIXTH SENSE
Superpower: Electroreception
Sharks can pick up on electrical signals coming off twitching muscle fibers in the water. Jelly-filled pits on their snout guide them straight to dinner.

Sharks are so sensitive to electric currents, they often chomp through underwater cables.

Pit organs pick up temperature variations as tiny as one one-thousandth of a degree.

HEAT SEEKER
Superpower: Heat vision
Pit vipers have pits in their nostrils that allow them to "see" infrared light. It means they can locate warm-blooded victims before a deadly strike.

UV-VISION
Superpower: UV-vision
Insects' eyes can see in ultraviolet (UV) as well as normal (visible) light, and the plant world knows this. If you could view your garden with "UV-specs," flowers would reveal the invisible patterns that guide pollinating insects toward them.

SPIDERY SENSES

Superpower: Early-warning system

Arthropods—insects, millipedes, spiders, crabs, and lobsters—have an outer shell that bristles with sensitive hairs and slits that allow the animal to sense air currents and its own movement.

Hair-trigger sensors allow flies to control their flight and avoid being swatted.

THE NOSE KNOWS

Superpower: Vein-o-vision

A vampire bat's snout is loaded with the same chemicals that alert you that your drink is hot. Heat-sensing cells detect warm blood flowing in veins beneath the skin.

ODD-LOOKING ANIMAL

The platypus looks as if it is made from spare animal parts. This Australian mammal looks like a mole, lays eggs, and has a bill like a duck! The bill is very sophisticated: The platypus must close its eyes and nostrils while diving in murky water, so the bill picks up on weak electrical fields put out by other animals. This makes the platypus the only mammal with electroreception. The bill is also packed with sensitive cells that can detect the smallest movement of its invertebrate prey.

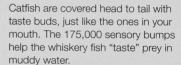

LAP IT UP

Superpower: Full-body supertongue

Catfish are covered head to tail with taste buds, just like the ones in your mouth. The 175,000 sensory bumps help the whiskery fish "taste" prey in muddy water.

THE EYES HAVE IT

ANIMALS HAVE SOME MIND-BLOWING WAYS OF SEEING THE WORLD. HERE'S LOOKING AT SOME OF THE MOST AMAZING EYES IN NATURE.

BAR-EYED
Goats have horizontal pupils. This gives them a 330-degree field of vision, compared to your 185-degree field of vision.

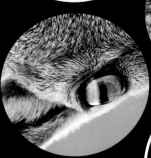

STONE-COLD STARE
The eyes of a West Indian fuzzy chiton rock—literally! This heavily armored marine mollusk has lenses made of limestone.

EYES ON STALKS
Snails have light-sensitive "eye spots" on the tips of their tentacles. They can wave their tentacles to "look" in any direction.

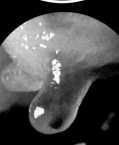

FIXED VISION
An owl's eyes are fixed in their sockets for steady vision in flight. Because it can't move its eyes, an owl's neck rotates through 270°.

BLINK! GULP!
Frogs shut their eyes when swallowing. Pushing them back into the head helps them swallow their insect dinners.

CONE-EYED CHAMELEONS
A chameleon's eyelids cover everything but the pupil. Each eye can move independently to follow and focus on prey.

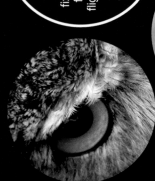

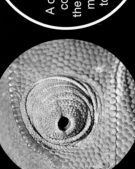

SPIDEY SENSES

Some jumping spiders have eight eyes to give them 360-degree vision. Some can even detect invisible ultraviolet light.

NIGHT VISION

Insects have compound eyes, made up of thousands of lenses. The giant Indian carpenter bee can pick out colors at night.

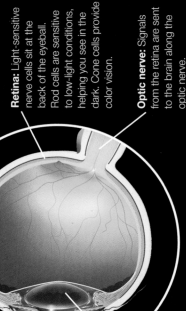

GIANT EYES

For life in the depths of the ocean, with barely any sunlight, a colossal squid's eyes grow to the size of a human head!

WINKY FACE

Cuttlefish pupils form a W shape. This strange shape actually improves their eyesight in dimmly lit waters.

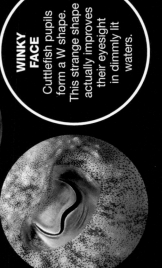

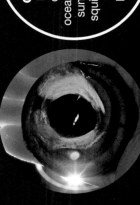

Iris: This ring of muscle allows more, or less, light into the eye, depending on the light conditions outside the eye. It also gives you your eye color.

Lens: Focuses incoming light onto light-sensitive cells at the back of the eye.

Retina: Light-sensitive nerve cells sit at the back of the eyeball. Rod cells are sensitive to low-light conditions, helping you see in the dark. Cone cells provide color vision.

Optic nerve: Signals from the retina are sent to the brain along the optic nerve.

EYE EYE!

Most mammals' eyes are built to the same plan: The pupil is just a hole that lets light into the eyeballs. Large predators that chase down their prey tend to have round pupils. Vertical slits help smaller predators accurately judge the distance to their prey. Some animals have such dark eyes, it can be hard to spot the pupil. The drawing on the right shows how the human eye works.

TASTE SENSATION!

You may have heard that different parts of the tongue taste different things. This is not true. Yes, there are receptor cells that taste different flavors, but all parts of the tongue can relish them.

Taste receptors are nerve endings that have a chemical reaction to particular chemicals in food. There are five different tastes—sweet, salty, sour, and bitter are the first four. The fifth taste is called "umami," which is a savory flavor.

DID YOU KNOW?

Chemicals can mess with your taste buds. The sodium lauryl sulfate in toothpaste reduces sweet sensations, making orange juice taste super tangy.

TASTY!

FIND A MIRROR. LOOK INTO IT AND STICK OUT YOUR TONGUE. BEHOLD A TRUE MARVEL! THIS PINK, SLOBBERY, WAGGLING GIZMO HELPS YOU BREATHE, SWALLOW, TALK, AND TASTE! SAY *AHHHH!*

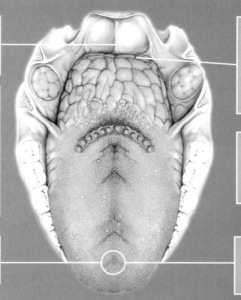

Taste buds are also found on the roof of the mouth and in the throat.

The tongue is the only muscle attached at just one end. With no internal skeleton, it works like an elephant's trunk or an octopus's tentacle.

Taste buds have tiny holes on their surfaces. Food dissolved in spit washes into the pores where special taste-receptor cells send the "flavor data" to the brain.

Although it's often called a single muscle, your tongue is actually made up of eight interwoven muscles.

Most taste buds are on the tip of the tongue.

Each taste bud has around 50 to 150 taste-receptor cells.

The world's longest human tongue measures a taste-tastic 3.97 in (10.1 cm) long, from tip to closed top lip. It belongs to Nick Stoeberl of Salinas, California.

Taste buds are not visible to the human eye. They are clustered around tiny bumps, called papillae, found on the top surface and sides of the tongue.

Papillae also contain serous glands, which produce some of the saliva juice that builds in your mouth.

A person's tongue has between 2,000 and 10,000 taste buds!

PIG OUT
CHAPTER 4

DID YOU KNOW?

A panda's favorite food is bamboo, but the animal lacks the proper microbes in its guts to break down plant matter. It means that pandas have to eat pounds and pounds of the plant each day to meet their energy needs. Turn to page **71** to find out how much they eat.

ROLL UP, ROLL UP!

DUNG BEETLES HAVE A HUGE FONDNESS FOR FECES. THEY MAKE QUICK WORK OF MANURE, WHICH THEY USE TO RAISE THEIR LITTLE LARVAE.

DELICIOUS, NUTRITIOUS!

Large grazing animals, such as elephants, rhinos, and cows, munch vast amounts of vegetation. Much of it passes through the body undigested, so dung contains heaps of good food for bugs and their grubs.

FRESH IS BEST

Dung beetles use their sense of smell to find fresh poop. They arrive in large numbers. Roughly 3 lb (1.5 kg) of elephant feces can be sliced, diced, and carted off in a few hours.

Adult beetles slurp up juicy moisture from the heap.

BEETLING AWAY

There are three main types of dung beetles:

"Rollers" are beetle species that create large dung balls. They roll them away using their powerful back legs. The female lays her eggs in the dung.

"Tunnelers" land on feces and dig down underneath it, dragging dung down into their cozy home.

"Dwellers" dispense with the hard work of rolling or digging, and simply make their palace in a poop pile instead.

Dung beetles walk backward when rolling dung, using their hind legs to do all the pushing.

Larvae tuck into solid poop.

⚛ STARGAZER

Once a "roller" has its ball of dung, it leaves the heap as quickly as it can to avoid other beetles trying to steal it. Since the quickest route is to roll in a straight line, the beetle uses the sun or the moon to navigate. On moonless nights, African dung beetles use the Milky Way to get their bearings.

69

ONE-TRACK MIND

IF YOU COULD EAT ONE THING FOR THE REST OF YOUR LIFE, WHAT WOULD IT BE? PIZZA? ICE CREAM? BRUSSELS SPROUTS? SOME ANIMALS ARE FUSSY EATERS AND WILL ONLY TOUCH ONE FOOD.

CUDDLY, CUTE KOALAS
These famously sleepy Australian marsupials live in eucalyptus forests. There are more than 600 species of eucalyptus trees. Koalas choose from around 40 types of those—and eat little else.

Eucalyptus leaves take a lot of energy to break down. Koalas sleep for up to 20 hours, to allow time to digest their difficult diet.

AN EARLY START
From about 22 weeks, a baby koala eats "pap," a special type of poop produced by its mom. It contains microorganisms that help digest eucalyptus leaves and prepare the baby koala for a lifetime of eating the real thing.

EATS SHOOTS AND LEAVES

This black-and-white bear from China loves bamboo. It eats pretty much nothing else. A tiny part of its diet is made of other plants and the meat of small rodents.

Pandas chow down up to 84 lb (38 kg) of bamboo per day.

EGGS-ELLENT EATING

African and Indian egg-eating snakes sneak into bird nests to feast on eggs. A keen sense of smell tells them which eggs are good and which are bad.

Muscles in the snake's throat push sharp spine bones against the delicate shell to make it crack.

SLOW FOOD

The snail kite mostly eats apple snails. This bird's beak is slender and wickedly curved—perfect for picking out its slimy prey from their shells.

71

MY BIG MOUTH

A RETICULATED PYTHON CAN EASILY TAKE A RABBIT INTO ITS SOCK-LIKE MOUTH AND SWALLOW IT WHOLE. THESE HUMUNGOUS JUNGLE SERPENTS MOSTLY EAT SMALL MAMMALS, BUT CAN ALSO STRETCH THEIR JAWS TO FIT PIGS AND EVEN ANTELOPE!

SIESTA TIME
Once a python has finished eating its prey, it slides off to rest in a warm place. Digesting a big meal takes a long while, so pythons don't eat very often.

MAIN SQUEEZE
A python kills by constriction. It loops its body around its prey, tightening its hold each time the victim breathes out. This cuts off the blood flow to the brain, causing all bodily functions to shut down, and the prey dies.

DOWN THE HATCH
Like all snakes, pythons lack chewing teeth, so they swallow their prey whole. Their snacks almost always go down headfirst.

DID YOU KNOW?
The reticulated python is one of the few snakes large enough to swallow a human. In 2017, villagers on the Indonesian island of Sulawesi captured and killed a 23-ft-long (7 m) reticulated python. Inside the creature was a 25-year-old man, entirely whole, fully clothed, and sadly dead.

AMBUSH PREDATOR
A reticulated python's camouflage markings allow it to remain almost invisible in the jungle.

JAWS OF DEATH
A python's jaw swings wide open to eat meals. The jaw comes in two pieces. With no chin bone, the two pieces are connected by a stretchy ligament.

TOOTHY GRIP
A python has around 100 razor-sharp, backward-curving teeth arranged in several rows. They help the snake to grip an animal as it goes into its mouth.

JUNGLE GIANT
The record length for a reticulated python (in captivity) is 25 ft, 2 in (7.67 m). It is the longest snake in the world.

SIZE ERROR
In 2005, Florida rangers found a Burmese python that had burst while trying to swallow an alligator. It is possible the alligator clawed at the stomach from the inside.

73

CHEWING THE CUD

COWS TURN GRASS INTO MILK. THEY ACHIEVE THIS REMARKABLE FEAT WITH THE HELP OF A LARGE STOMACH THAT IS DIVIDED INTO FOUR COMPARTMENTS. THE PROCESS INVOLVES FIVE MAIN STAGES.

1. RUMEN AROUND
The rumen is the largest of the four stomach compartments. Chewed-up plants are sloshed about, soaked, and softened here. Microbes in the rumen help break down the greenery.

DEDICATED DIGESTER
Cows are herbivores—they eat plants. To get the goodness out of their food, plant-eaters must break down tough cellulose in a plant's cell walls. That's why they have a four-part stomach.

Cows must chew food multiple times to digest tough plant fibers.

4. FILTER TIME
The cow's grassy mush passes through to the omasum. The food is held here while fluids pass through. Bacteria continue to break down the grass.

3. MORE CHEWING
The reticulum shoots small balls of softened food back up the cow's throat. The cow patiently re-chews and re-swallows the food, now called the "cud."

2. IN THE POCKET

The food passes from the rumen to the reticulum, a small muscley pouch at the front of the stomach.

1

NUMBER-MUNCHER

32 teeth

24 molars at the back of the mouth

8 bottom incisors at the front of the mouth

0 top front teeth

5. ABO-MASH-UP

The cow's stomach is finally ready to absorb food. The partially digested mulch passes into the cow's true stomach (the abomasum), which produces stomach acid and chemicals that help digestion. These extract nutrients from the food.

An average cow produces as many as 112 half-pint (235 ml) glasses of milk every day.

WHALE WATCH

THERE ARE TWO GROUPS OF WHALES—TOOTHED AND BALEEN. THEY ALL HAVE THE SAME STREAMLINED SHAPE, BUT THERE ARE DIFFERENCES IN THE WAY THE TWO GROUPS TAKE THEIR FOOD.

TOOTHED WHALES

0   10   20   30   40   50   60   70   80   90   100   feet

Sperm Whale

LARGEST TOOTHER
Sperm whale
Length: 70 ft (21 m)
Weight: 59 t (54 mt)

Killer Whale

Cuvier's Beaked Whale

There are 67 toothed whale species.

BIG EATERS

A large male sperm whale can eat 2,660 lb (1,200 kg) of squid a day. A big blue whale can swallow up to 1,100 lb (500 kg) of krill in a single massive mouthful.

TOOTHY TIME
Toothed whales are agile hunters, chasing and capturing prey, sometimes in groups. They zero in on their fishy targets using echolocating clicks and catch a wide variety of sea life in their teeth, including fish, squid, and crabs.

DEEP AND MYSTERIOUS
Sperm whales can dive down to 3,280 ft (1 km) and stay underwater for over an hour. A sperm whale's huge head is full of a strange white oil called spermaceti. No one is sure what it is for.

DEFINING CHARACTERISTICS
Toothed whales have a single blowhole. Males are usually bigger than females and they live in complex social groups.

BALEEN WHALES

100 90 80 70 60 50 40 30 20 10 0

Blue Whale (gulper)

Bowhead Whale (skimmer)

Gray Whale (rooter)

MUSTACHIOED MOUNTAINS
Baleen whales include the blue whale. A baleen's "mustache" is its fringe of flat baleen plates around the upper jaw.

DEFINING CHARACTERISTICS
Besides the "mustache," these ocean giants have two blowholes. They live in small groups. Females are usually longer than males.

BIGGEST BALEEN
Blue whale
Length: 100 ft (30 m)
Weight: 150 t (136 mt)

FILTER FEEDING
Baleen plates filter out food from seawater. Gulpers take a huge mouthful of water and use their tongue to force the water back out through the baleen. This traps plankton, krill, or small fish on the inside of the bristles, where the tongue works them back to the gullet. Skimmers swim with their mouths open. Bottom feeders (rooters) sift treats from seafloor mud.

There are only 12 species of baleen whales.

PIG OUT

77

A VARIED DIET

PEOPLE ARE OMNIVOROUS AND NEED TO EAT A VARIED DIET TO STAY HEALTHY. TAKE A LOOK AT YOUR PLATE NEXT TIME YOU EAT. DOES IT LOOK ANYTHING LIKE THIS? IF SO, CONGRATULATIONS: YOU ARE GETTING A HEALTHY, BALANCED MEAL!

More than half of our diet comes from maize, wheat, and rice.

OMNI-EATERS

Omnivores, like humans, are the animal kingdom's flexible feeders. They eat whatever food is available—plants and meat. This kind of feeding strategy has advantages, such as allowing for an alternative if one food type is scarce.

Whole grains

Whole-wheat bread and pasta, and brown rice get a big thumbs-up in this section. Try to limit refined grains, such as white bread and white rice.

Water

Drink lots of water, but steer clear of sugary drinks like soda. Milk and fruit juices are fine in moderation.

Protein

Healthy meats include fish and chicken. Remember that red meat and cheese contain lots of saturated fats. Avoid bacon, cured meats, and processed meats.

Oils

Healthy oils include olive and avocado oil. Keep an eye on how much butter you use, and avoid margarine.

Fruit

Hooray for fruit! Make sure you eat plenty of fresh fruit of all colors.

Veggies

Load up on veggies—the more the better! Variety is the key. Remember, French fries and potatoes don't count.

⚛ TOOTHY TOOLS

Tackling different foods requires a versatile set of tools. Many mammal omnivores, including we humans, have specialized teeth. These include sharp, biting teeth for tearing and ripping meat and vegetable stalks, and flat molars for crunching and grinding grains and tough foods.

LOOK INSIDE

WHAT ARE HUMANS MADE OF? SOME SAY SUGAR AND SPICE, OTHERS SAY SPIT AND BILE. HERE'S THE SKINNY ON WHAT MAKES YOU, YOU.

SHIFT YOUR BONES

The heaviest part of anyone's body is their muscles. Added together, your bones account for around one-seventh of your body weight. This makes sense when you think about it—any heavier and you'd have trouble moving around!

The body contains about 1.5 gal (5.5 L) of blood.

An average person's body holds about 0.2 mg of gold, most of it in the blood.

Around 99% of your body's calcium and 85% of its phosphorus are in your bones.

PERCENTAGE OF BODY WEIGHT

Muscles — 31.56%

Other body tissues — 17.42%

Skeleton — 14.84%

Fat — 13.63%

Skin — 7.81%

Lungs — 4.15%

Liver — 3.41%

Brain, spinal cord, and nerve trunks — 2.52%

PERCENTAGE OF BODY WEIGHT

2.07%
Digestive tract

0.86%
Digestive organs

0.8%
Undigested food

0.69%
Heart

0.15%
Digestive juices

0.06%
Teeth

0.03%
Hair

IT'S ELEMENTARY!

About 60 different chemical elements are found in the human body. Just four of those account for over 96 percent of your mass, joined together in the various chemical substances that your body uses. By far the largest component is water (H_2O)—nearly two-thirds of your body weight.

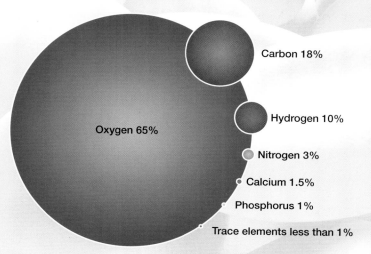

Oxygen 65%

Carbon 18%

Hydrogen 10%

Nitrogen 3%

Calcium 1.5%

Phosphorus 1%

Trace elements less than 1%

Some "trace elements," such as selenium and iron, can be fatal in higher concentrations, yet we cannot live without them. Iron, for example, is essential for transporting oxygen in the blood.

On average, a human body contains 7,000,000,000,000,000,000,000,000,000 (7 billion, billion, billion) tiny atoms.

81

SUPERTECH

CHAPTER 5

DID YOU KNOW?

Hexagons fit together without gaps between them. Their shape allows bees to store the largest amount of honey using the least amount of wax. This makes them ideal for building honeycomb (see pages **86–87**).

EARLY-WARNING SYSTEMS

11

IT'S EARLY MORNING IN
THE KALAHARI DESERT,
SOUTHERN AFRICA. THE
MEERKAT MOB ARE OUT
OF THEIR BURROWS AND
LOOKING FOR BREAKFAST.
TO KEEP THEM SAFE, A FEW
MEERKATS STAND GUARD.

MINI MARVELS
At around 11 in (28 cm), a
meerkat stands as tall as
a 12-in (30 cm) ruler.

DID YOU KNOW?
A meerkat can spot an eagle
in the sky from a distance of
1,000 ft (305 m).

GUARD DUTY
Meerkats have developed a
sentry system for spotting
danger in the African skies,
and to prevent surprise
ground attacks while they
are looking for food. For
these critters, many eyes
make light work.

Meerkats live in
cooperative colonies
of up to 40 members.

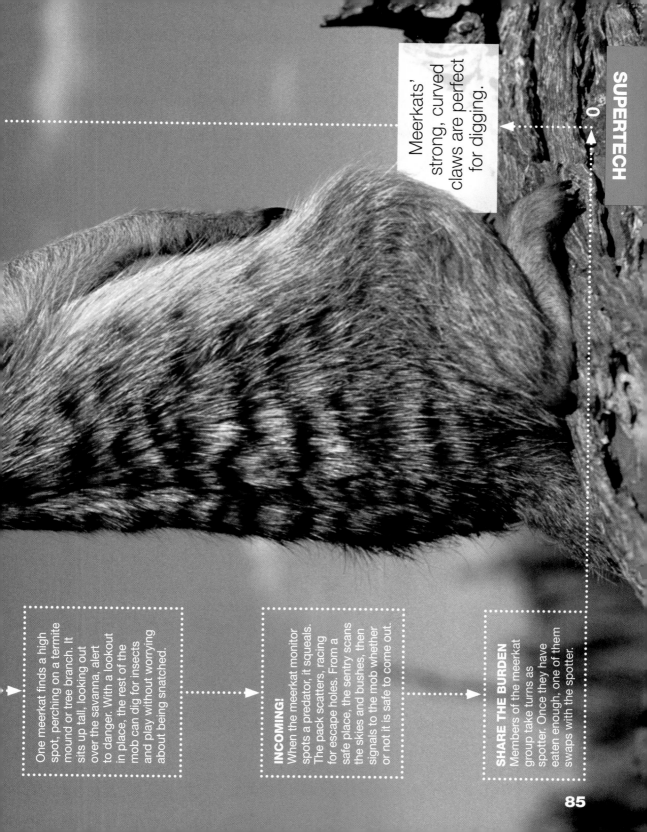

Meerkats' strong, curved claws are perfect for digging.

One meerkat finds a high spot, perching on a termite mound or tree branch. It sits up tall, looking out over the savanna, alert to danger. With a lookout in place, the rest of the mob can dig for insects and play without worrying about being snatched.

INCOMING!
When the meerkat monitor spots a predator, it squeals. The pack scatters, racing for escape holes. From a safe place, the sentry scans the skies and bushes, then signals to the mob whether or not it is safe to come out.

SHARE THE BURDEN
Members of the meerkat group take turns as spotter. Once they have eaten enough, one of them swaps with the spotter.

HIVE MIND

WORKER BEES ZIP AND ZOOM FROM FLOWER TO FLOWER, TRAVELING THE EQUIVALENT OF TWO TO THREE TIMES AROUND THE WORLD FOR EACH POUND (454 G) OF HONEY.

HIVE AND SURVIVE
In nests, honeybees build wax combs of stacked hexagonal cells. They fill the cells with nectar. The queen lays her eggs in the cells and the combs become a nursery for raising bee larvae.

PERFECT SYMMETRY
Honeycomb cells are perfect hexagons—all sides are equal. Each cell is exactly the same size, which means that all bees can work at the same time, building their own cells to slot together with the rest.

THE ONE AND ONLY
A colony has just one queen bee. She eats a white cream called royal jelly. During the spring, she lays more than 1,000 eggs a day.

DID YOU KNOW?
A honeybee hive may contain as many as 80,000 bees.

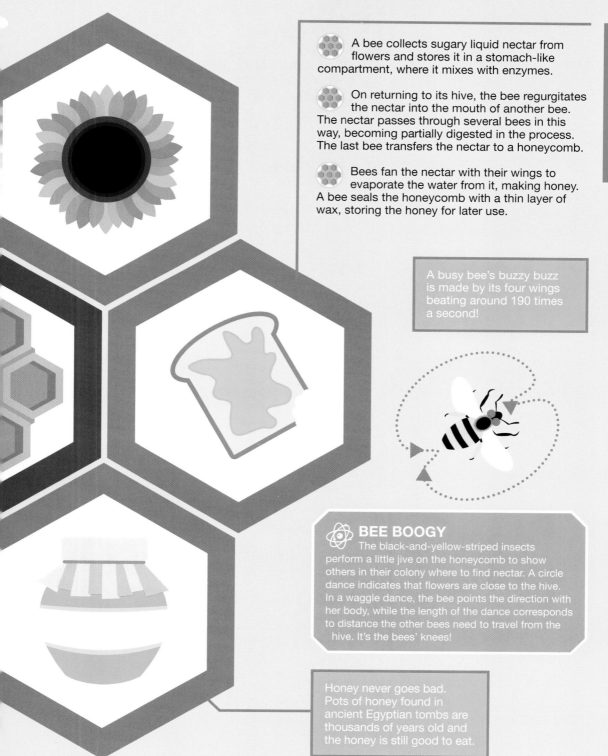

A bee collects sugary liquid nectar from flowers and stores it in a stomach-like compartment, where it mixes with enzymes.

On returning to its hive, the bee regurgitates the nectar into the mouth of another bee. The nectar passes through several bees in this way, becoming partially digested in the process. The last bee transfers the nectar to a honeycomb.

Bees fan the nectar with their wings to evaporate the water from it, making honey. A bee seals the honeycomb with a thin layer of wax, storing the honey for later use.

A busy bee's buzzy buzz is made by its four wings beating around 190 times a second!

BEE BOOGY

The black-and-yellow-striped insects perform a little jive on the honeycomb to show others in their colony where to find nectar. A circle dance indicates that flowers are close to the hive. In a waggle dance, the bee points the direction with her body, while the length of the dance corresponds to distance the other bees need to travel from the hive. It's the bees' knees!

Honey never goes bad. Pots of honey found in ancient Egyptian tombs are thousands of years old and the honey is still good to eat.

TOOLING AROUND

HUMANS AREN'T THE ONLY TOOL USERS. MANY ANIMALS FIND WAYS TO USE OBJECTS AS TOOLS, TOO. SOME BIRDS USE STONES TO BREAK OPEN HARD FOODS, AND ELEPHANTS BUST THROUGH ELECTRIC FENCES BY DROPPING STONES ON THEM. SOME CRAFTY CREATURES NOT ONLY FIND THINGS TO USE AS TOOLS, BUT EVEN ALTER THEM TO MAKE THEM FUNCTION BETTER!

MONKEY BUSINESS

Chimps are champs at using tools. The primates crack nuts with stones, and use sticks to fish for tasty termites and to dip for honey. Chimps chew sticks to make water-absorbent brushes for getting long, cool drinks.

Sticks and stones

SEAFOOD SPECIALIST

Sea otters love shellfish, but snails, crabs, and clams have shells for protection. A smart sea otter swims on its back, balancing a stone on its belly. It whacks shells against the rock until they break.

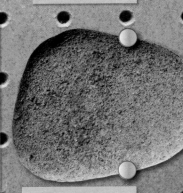

Shell-cracking rock

COCO-NUTS!
A veined octopus carries its own portable shelter. This mollusk digs up and cleans out coconut shell halves before scampering across patches of seabed where there is nowhere to hide from predators.

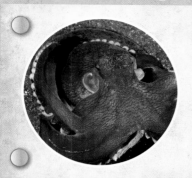

Coconut cover

SPIKY FELLOW
The woodpecker finch is a small bird that likes to eat grubs (wormlike insect larvae). When it finds a juicy treat, the bird flies off to a cactus and returns with a spine with which to spike its tasty dinner.

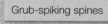

Grub-spiking spines

TREATS FROM TRAFFIC
In Japan, canny carrion crows take advantage of passing cars to break open walnut shells. They have even learned to use the crosswalk!

Nut-cracking tire

BRAIN

YOUR BRAIN KEEPS ALL PARTS OF YOUR BODY WORKING TOGETHER IN PERFECT STEP. THIS AMAZINGLY COMPLEX THINKING MACHINE LETS YOU MAKE SENSE OF THE WORLD, BUT HOW IT DOES THIS IS STILL A MYSTERY.

CEREBRAL CORTEX
Your brain's "gray matter" is its bumpy top layer: If its wrinkles and creases were flattened out, it would cover 2.5 sq ft (0.23 m²). The cerebral cortex has four main lobes—each with areas that play different roles.

FRONTAL LOBE
The command and control center that coordinates all parts of your brain.

PREFRONTAL CORTEX
Handles problem-solving, decision-making, planning, recognizing emotions, and complex thought.

BROCA'S AREA
Production of speech.

SUBCORTEX
Beneath the cerebral cortex are many small regions that monitor your body's internal state and control sleeping and waking, hunger and thirst, and fear and feelings.

APPEARING SMART
What makes humans smart is one of the biggest unexplained mysteries. Scientists think that intelligence may be linked to the number of connections in the brain—this hugely complex organ contains about 200 trillion connections between brain cells—and also to which parts of the brain are being connected.

TEMPORAL LOBE
Hearing is controlled in this part of your brain. It also forms and stores memories.

90

POWER

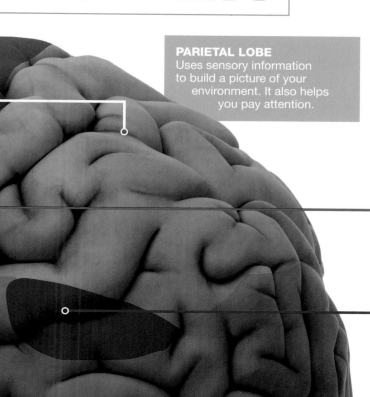

PARIETAL LOBE
Uses sensory information to build a picture of your environment. It also helps you pay attention.

Your brain is divided into two halves joined by a thick bundle of nerves.

MOTOR CORTEX
Plans and executes complex movements.

WERNICKE'S AREA
Language comprehension center.

OCCIPITAL LOBE
This part of your brain is dedicated to receiving and analyzing information from your eyes.

CEREBELLUM
A mini-brain hangs off the back of your brain. It coordinates your movements. Although only the size of a fist, it contains about 70 billion neurons.

BRAINSTEM
The brainstem automatically controls your critical body systems, such as breathing and swallowing, your heart rate and blood pressure.

The average adult brain weighs 2.95 lb (1.34 kg)—about the size of a small chicken.

WHERE WE LIVE

WE HUMANS MAY BE OUTNUMBERED BY INSECTS AND OUTWEIGHED BY BACTERIA, BUT UNLIKE INSECTS AND BACTERIA, WE HAVE MODIFIED ALMOST EVERY PART OF THE PLANET.

WHERE IN THE WORLD?

There are nearly **7.6 billion** humans on the planet. By 2024, the world population is predicted to hit 8 billion. Most live in Asia—China, with 1.4 billion, and India, with 1.3 billion, are the two countries that have the most people.

DID YOU KNOW?

Some countries have aging populations because people are living longer and not as many babies are being born. Today, in Japan, more adult diapers are sold than baby diapers.

Asia 60%

7,515,000,000

Europe 10%

Africa 17%

South America and the Caribbean 9%

North America and Oceania 6%

If everyone were to stand next to each other, the entire population of the world could fit into an area the size of Los Angeles.

In 2016, there were 31 megacities of over 10 million people.

CITY LIVING

Cities make up just three percent of Earth's land, but more than half the people on Earth live in them. What's more, one out of every five people lives in a city with a population of over one million.

CALL OF THE WILD

Over four-fifths of Earth's land has been affected by humans. Crops cover 11 percent of the land, but scientists believe that this takes up just one-third of the land that could be used to grow food.

One-quarter of the world's people are under 15 years old.

The most densely populated country is Monaco, with nearly 00,000 people per square mile (2.6 sq km).

WE'VE GOT THE POWER!

HUMANKIND'S GREATEST LEAPS FORWARD HAVE BEEN FUELED BY NEW SOURCES OF POWER.

c.500–400 B.C.E.

ANIMAL POWER
Oxen and donkeys are used to power grinding mills.

FIRE
c.1.4 million years ago

Humans learn to control fire to clear fields. Cooking food on fires allows for a richer diet. Fire aids survival in cold places.

c.400–350 B.C.E.

WATER WHEEL
The energy of running water powers mills, water pumps, and other simple machines.

BOOM!
c.900 C.E.

Chinese alchemists discover gunpowder.

FLINTS AND BOW DRILLS
Fire-starting gadgets are the must-have tools for Stone Age folks.

WINDMILL
c.1100

The ability to grind grain using wind power, known in medieval Europe and Persia (modern-day Iran).

c.3000 B.C.E.

METAL WORKING
Hotter furnaces extract metal from rocks. New metal tools and weapons replace stone hardware.

STEAM ENGINE
1712

Piston-driven engines take over from muscle power. They can run forever without getting tired.

1800

ELECTRIC BATTERY
Alessandro Volta invents a reliable source of electrical current.

1821 ELECTRIC MOTOR
Michael Faraday discovers how to convert electricity into motion.

1937 TURBOJET
Modern air travel becomes possible thanks to Frank Whittle's jet engine.

1879 LIGHT BULB
Replaces gas lighting in factories operating around-the-clock with shift workers.

1942 NUCLEAR POWER
The world enters the nuclear age with the first nuclear fission reactor, which converts mass by splitting atoms to create energy.

1886 GASOLINE ENGINE
The first automobiles powered by oil go into production.

1954 SOLAR POWER
Bell Labs invents the first photovoltaic cells. They convert light into electricity.

1887 WIND TURBINE
Electricity is generated by wind power for the first time.

1961 MEGA-BOOM!
Test of the world's largest nuclear bomb—the Soviet Union's Tsar Bomba—releases 10 times the energy of all the regular explosives used in World War II.

1896 RADIOACTIVITY
A strange new energy source is discovered by French scientist Henri Becquerel.

2012 WORLD'S LARGEST HYDROELECTRIC POWER STATION
The Three Gorges Dam in China generates the same energy as burning 55 million tons of coal per year.

COMPUTER TALK

COMPUTERS CHATTER AROUND THE CLOCK, LINKED TOGETHER IN VAST NETWORKS. MILLIONS OF MACHINES SEND INFORMATION WHIZZING AROUND THE WORLD, CONNECTING PEOPLE INSTANTLY.

ONLINE WORLD

Less than half the people on the planet are connected to the Internet. This global network of computers allows us to communicate with each other via email and voice and video calls, and to share our lives on social media. Computer web servers allow us to store information, shop, stream movies, play games, and

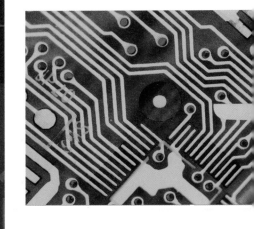

SPECIAL DELIVERY

Information sent over the Internet is broken into small packets. Each packet contains the address of the computer sending it, as well as the address of the destination computer, plus instructions on how it all fits together.

TOTALLY WIRED
Submarine cables that run under the sea connect countries to each other. Hundreds of thousands of miles of wires, some as thick as a soda can, carry the world's Internet traffic.

The longest submarine cable in the world is 24,000 miles (39,000 km) long and reaches 33 countries on four continents.

When the packets arrive at their destination, the information they contain is reassembled in the correct order.

Packets can take different routes through the Internet,

always finding the fastest, and avoiding traffic. They might go

via a local web server, or one on the other side of the world.

ONES AND ZEROS
Computers communicate using binary code—zeros and ones joined together in strings.

BIT
The smallest unit of data. A "0" or a "1" represents a Yes or a No.

BYTE
1 byte = 8 bits
A byte represents one character. It takes about 10 bytes to make a word and 100 bytes would make a short sentence.

KILOBYTE
1 KB = 1,000 bytes
A kilobyte is about the same as a paragraph of writing.

MEGABYTE
1 MB = 1,000 KB
A megabyte is the equivalent of a short book.

GIGABYTE
1 GB = 1,000 MB
1 gigabyte could contain the contents of a shelf of books 10 yards (9 m) long.

TERABYTE
1 TB = 1,000 GB
10 terabytes would hold the entire collection of the Library of Congress.

PETABYTE
1 PB = 1,000 TB
Google processes about 20 PB every day.

EXABYTE
1 EB = 1,000 PB
All the words ever spoken by humankind add up to around 5 EB.

ZETTABYTE
1 ZB = 1,000 EB
About the same as 250 billion DVDs' worth of data.

YOTTABYTE
1 YB = 1,000 ZB
The entire Internet takes up about a yottabyte.

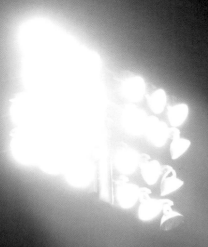

1

BOLD AND BRASSY
The whistle body is cut from sheets of solid brass, just 400ths of an inch thick (1 mm). A punch press slices through the metal, like a cookie cutter through dough, cutting out the top and sides of the whistle.

HOW WHISTLES ARE MADE

LOUD AND SHRILL, A WHISTLE BLAST IS EASILY HEARD OVER THE NOISE OF THE PLAYERS AND THE ROAR OF THE CROWD. IT'S THE SOUND OF A TOUCHDOWN OR A PENALTY KICK IN THE LAST MINUTE OF A WORLD CUP GAME. LET'S HAVE A "PEEP" AT HOW WHISTLES ARE MADE!

DID YOU KNOW?
The first time a referee used a whistle was in 1878, in a soccer game between Nottingham Forest FC and Sheffield Norfolk FC, in England. Before this, refs used to wave a handkerchief —not quite the same effect!

5

THE HUMAN TOUCH
A worker snaps the two whistle halves together. The bottom half stops short, leaving a gap on top of the whistle—the air slot.

PRESSING BUSINESS
A second press folds up the "ears" to make the sides of the whistle's barrel.

CLEAN AS A WHISTLE
A third press forms the whistle's lower part from a separate brass strip.

4

FOURTH AND FINAL
A final factory press finishes the whistle's circular underside to form the barrel.

SNUG FIT
A machine applies solder (a type of metal) to six spots, and the whistle passes through a gas flame. The solder melts and runs freely through the seams, sealing them. A blast of cold air solidifies the solder.

IT'S A BLAST!
A ½-in (13 mm) ball puts the trill in the whistle's toot. The ball squashes to fit through the air slot and regains its shape once inside.

Ball made of synthetic cork, which does not absorb moisture.

HEY, YOU!

IMAGINE IF YOU COULD ONLY CONTACT FRIENDS WHO LIVE FAR AWAY BY SHOUTING OR WAVING YOUR ARMS!

From early times, people used low notes (drums) or high notes (yodeling), which travel farther than speech. Electricity changed how we communicate over long distances. In 1800, Italian Alessandro Volta invented the electric battery, allowing people to send reliable electric currents along wires. The currents could be used to send messages—at first simple on–off pulses, then human speech and pictures. More inventions followed, creating today's amazingly interconnected world.

2000s SOCIAL MEDIA

Facebook, YouTube, Twitter, and Tumblr allow us all to share our thoughts with other people. As with drumming or yodeling, one person can reach many others at the same time.

1990s EMAIL

Although email was invented in the 1970s, this virtually instant communication took off in the 1990s. Today, 3.1 million emails are sent every second.

1983 CELL PHONE

The first commercial cell phone sold for $3,995 and weighed 1.75 lb (0.8 kg). Today more people own cell phones than have flush toilets!

1962 COMMUNICATIONS SATELLITE

Satellites can get a message to the other side of the world at the speed of light, using radio waves beamed to and from stations on the ground.

1876 TELEPHONE

Alexander Graham Bell introduced the first working telephone in 1876. Its range and power were improved by the invention of the microphone in 1877, which gave a clearer sound.

1860 PONY EXPRESS

Mail traveled nearly 2,000 miles (3,200 km) from Missouri to California, taking 10 days. Riders changed horses about every 10 miles (16 km), riding up to 100 miles (160 km) before passing the mail to the next rider.

1840s FAX

Just as the telephone can transmit sound waves via a line, the facsimile transmission could send a picture by breaking it down into tiny squares.

3000 B.C.E DRUMMING/ YODELING

Sound signals allow humans to communicate over long distances and different terrains: The sound of drumming moves through forests, while yodeling echoes across mountain valleys.

900 B.C.E FIRE SIGNALS

Smoke and fire have long been used to warn of danger, spread news, and gather people together.

400 B.C.E CARRIER PIGEON

With average speeds of 48 MPH (78 kmh), pigeons use Earth's magnetic field to navigate. The Persians were among the first to use carrier pigeons to send messages.

1700s SIGNAL FLAGS

At sea, sailors wave flags to communicate. By the 1690s, the British Navy had a system of flags that gave different orders, depending on color, number of flags, and location.

1824 BRAILLE

Louis Braille invented his alphabet of raised dots to help blind people to read and write. He was inspired by an earlier system of night reading, invented for Napoleon's soldiers but never used.

1838 MORSE CODE

Morse code reduced the alphabet to a series of dots and dashes that could be sent by wire using an electric current.

1844 TELEGRAPH

Samuel Morse's code was finally used over a cable 40 miles (64 km) long, connecting Baltimore, MD, and Washington, DC. The message? "What hath God wrought?"

FUTURE SCIENCE
THINKING ALOUD
Implants in the brain could one day send electrical impulses to a computer to help people who are totally paralyzed to communicate. Much more work is needed before the technology is ready for practical use.

AWESOME ELECTRIC

A NEW BREED OF HIGH-TECH VEHICLES IS QUIETLY TAKING OVER . . . SO QUIETLY, IN FACT, THAT YOU CAN BARELY HEAR THEM ROLLING UP BEHIND YOU! WELCOME TO THE AGE OF THE ELECTRIC CAR!

Electric cars convert up to 80 percent of a battery's energy; gas burners only achieve up to 26 percent efficiency.

UNDER THE HOOD
Instead of a gas-burning internal combustion engine, an electric car has an electric motor.

SHOCKING FUEL
The electrical energy that powers the motor is stored in batteries. Most electric cars use lithium-ion batteries — the same kind you find in a laptop or a cell phone. They are lighter than most batteries and are able to store lots of energy.

SPEEDY STARTERS

Whereas gas-powered engines get better at transferring power as their rotation speed increases, electric motors offer up near-full turning force the instant they switch on. This makes them incredibly zippy.

Top models go from 0 to 60 MPH (0 to 97 kmh) in just 2.39 seconds.

SMART ENERGY

The car's systems save on energy by using the brakes to recharge the batteries when the car slows down, and switching the engine off when the car stops.

FREE-RANGE FUTURE

Most electric vehicles travel for 80–100 miles (129–161 km) before they need recharging. They can be plugged in overnight at home. For longer journeys, charging stations can be found at some gas stations.

DIRTY SECRET?

Electric cars are said to have "zero emissions," but that doesn't mean they are non-polluting. Electric energy is only as clean as the power station that produces the electricity, and many power plants aren't emissions-free. Also, most people charge their cars at night, but the greenest power is generated during the day.

CLEAN DREAM

Because electric cars do not burn fuel, they produce no exhaust gases. "Zero emissions" cars release no carbon dioxide into the atmosphere, potentially making electric cars a better option for the planet!

DANGEROUS AND DEADLY

CHAPTER 6

DID YOU KNOW?

Fires need oxygen to stay lit. Since one-fifth of Earth's atmosphere is made of oxygen, there is always something burning somewhere on our planet. Yet there is one continent that never sees wildfires. Find out which on page **113**.

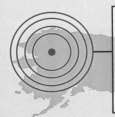

ALASKA 1964
Magnitude 9.2
Death toll: Estimated 131
Other damage: Four landslides and a tsunami caused $300–350 million worth of damage to property in Anchorage.

MOVERS AND SHAKERS

DURING AN EARTHQUAKE, THE GROUND TOSSES AND HEAVES LIKE A BUCKING BRONCO. CITIES SHAKE, ROADS SNAP, AND BUILDINGS CRUMBLE. HERE ARE THE TOP FIVE MOST POWERFUL EARTHQUAKES EVER RECORDED.

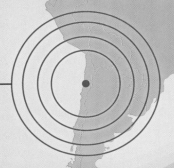

MOST POWERFUL EARTHQUAKE EVER
CHILE 1960
Magnitude 9.5
Death toll: Estimated 5,000
Other damage: The Valdivia earthquake left two million people homeless and created a tsunami that destroyed the Chilean port of Puerto Saavedra.

 ## WHAT CAUSES AN EARTHQUAKE?

In Japanese mythology, a gigantic catfish called Namazu makes the ground shake when he wiggles his mighty tail. In reality, scientists have discovered that our planet's surface rocks are broken into huge slabs, called plates, that shove and jostle each other. Most earthquakes happen at the plate edges where they crash into each other. A sudden slip along a crack in the ground releases energy that travels underground, making Earth's surface quake.

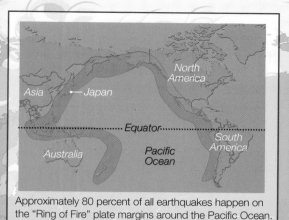

Approximately 80 percent of all earthquakes happen on the "Ring of Fire" plate margins around the Pacific Ocean.

RUSSIA 1952
Magnitude 9
Death toll: 0
Other damage: An earthquake in Kamchatka created destructive tsunami waves that reached Hawaii.

JAPAN 2011
Magnitude 9.1
Death toll: Estimated 15,853
Other damage: The tsunami caused a meltdown at the Fukushima nuclear plant.

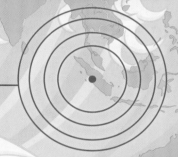

LONGEST RECORDED QUAKE

INDONESIA 2004
Magnitude 9.1
Death toll: Estimated 230,000
Other damage: The quake lasted 10 minutes. The resulting tsunami of December 26, 2004, affected 14 countries and devastated some of the world's poorest places.

Earthquake strength is measured on the Richter scale, which gives an idea of the amount of energy released. Magnitude 0–2 earthquakes are barely detectable, while those of magnitude 7–8 are major disasters.

Scientists detect about 500,000 earthquakes each year. One in five can be felt.

AWESOME ERUPTIONS

VOLCANOES ARE EARTH'S WAY OF SHOWING THE INCREDIBLE POWER THAT LIES BENEATH ITS SURFACE. THESE UNPREDICTABLE EXPLOSIONS OF FIRE AND FURY CAN BE DEVASTATING. HERE ARE SOME OF THE BIGGEST VOLCANIC ERUPTIONS THAT HAVE HAPPENED AROUND THE WORLD.

VEI 5
VERY LARGE

MOUNT ST. HELENS
USA
Notable eruption: 1980
This volcano exploded sideways, following the largest rock avalanche in recorded history. The eruption happened very suddenly. It killed 57 people, including a geologist who was monitoring the volcano's activity.

VEI 6
COLOSSAL

SANTA MARÍA
GUATEMALA
Pictured above: 2009
Largest eruption: 1902
Santa María mountain let rip with one of the 20th century's biggest booms. The eruption lasted 18 to 20 hours and tore an almost mile-wide (1.6 km) hole in the side of the mountain.

VEI 6
COLOSSAL

KRAKATOA
INDONESIA
Largest eruption: 1883
Map shows region today
A series of furious eruptions, the last of which completely obliterated the volcanic island. This Krakatoa eruption made the loudest sound ever recorded—a blast that reverberated four times around the planet.

Malaysia

Indian Ocean

Indonesia

Mt. Krakatoa

One in 20 people lives within the danger zone of an active volcano.

Each number on the Volcanic Explosivity Index (VEI) is 10 times greater than the one before.

There are around 1,500 active volcanoes in the world. About 50 of them erupt every year!

VEI 6
COLOSSAL

PINATUBO
LUZON, THE PHILIPPINES
Largest eruption: 1991
Mount Pinatubo, the second-largest eruption of the 20th century, blew an ash cloud more than 20 miles (32 km) high. Typhoon rain made the ash heavy as it settled. Roofs collapsed as a result, killing an estimated 300 people.

VEI 7
SUPER COLOSSAL

TAMBORA
INDONESIA
Pictured above: 2014
Largest eruption: 1815
The eruption blew about 4,000 ft (1,220 m) off the volcano's top. A "year without a summer" followed: Ash in the atmosphere brought down global temperatures, causing crop failures and famines.

VEI 8
MEGA COLOSSAL

YELLOWSTONE PARK
USA
Prehistoric eruptions
A supervolcano lies beneath America's iconic park. It saw three huge eruptions between 2.1 million years ago and 640,000 years ago. The last created the park's 1,350-square-mile (3,500 sq km) crater (pictured).

NEW LIFE
A new volcano has emerged where Krakatoa once stood. The rim of the new cone first appeared above sea level in 1927. Over time, this has grown into a volcanic island, now called Anak Krakatoa.

FORCE OF NATURE

AT AROUND 6 A.M. ON AUGUST 29, 2005, HURRICANE KATRINA MADE LANDFALL IN LOUISIANA. TWENTY-FOUR HOURS LATER, ONE OF THE DEADLIEST HURRICANES IN US HISTORY HAD LEFT NEW ORLEANS SHATTERED.

HURRICANE TIME

Hurricanes are areas of low pressure that form out at sea during the warm months of the year. Hurricane season is from early June to the end of November. Over any three years, two major tropical storms are expected to hit either the Gulf or Atlantic coasts of the United States. In 2017, Hurricanes Harvey and Irma made landfall with less than three weeks between them.

TROPICAL STORM STRENGTH

CAT 1
Wind speed 74–95 MPH
(119–153 kmh)
Winds cause
minimal damage

CAT 2
Wind speed 96–110 MPH
(154–177 kmh)
Widespread damage

CAT 3
Wind speed 111–129 MPH
(178–208 kmh)
Extensive damage

HURRICANE KATRINA IN NUMBERS

90,000 sq. m. (914,200 sq km) affected

353,000 homes damaged or destroyed

1,833 people killed

4/5 of New Orleans flooded

140 MPH (225 kmh) winds reached

HOW DO TROPICAL STORMS GET NAMED?

The World Meteorological Organization (WMO) gives each tropical storm a short, easy-to-remember name. They are chosen from a list of girls' and boys' names that rotates every six years. If a hurricane turns out to be particularly destructive, its name is withdrawn from the list. Here are some of the names that have been retired: Donna, Camille, Hugo, Andrew, Charley, Katrina.

SEVERE SURGES

The "storm surge" is a hurricane's most destructive element. A rapid rise of water pushed onshore by the powerful winds can result in water levels of over 15 ft (4.5 m), flooding low-lying coastal areas.

DID YOU KNOW?

The word "hurricane" comes from Hunraken, the Mayan storm god.

CAT 4
Wind speed 130–156 MPH (209–251 kmh)
Devastating damage

CAT 5
Wind speed 157+ MPH (252+ kmh)
Catastrophic damage

A full-blown hurricane releases the same amount of energy as a 10-megaton nuclear bomb exploding every 20 minutes!

WILDFIRE!

OUT-OF-CONTROL FIRES SWEEP ACROSS RURAL AREAS EVERY YEAR. THESE UNSTOPPABLE BLAZES ROAR ACROSS THE LAND, RAZING FORESTS AND HOMES TO THE GROUND, AND BRINGING INSTANT DEATH TO PLANTS, ANIMALS, AND EVEN HUMANS.

UP IN FLAMES

In many parts of the world, people use fires to clear new fields. Even lightning can spark a fire when vegetation is bone-dry. Oxygen in the air keeps flames burning. High temperatures heat up firewood and debris, making them burn more quickly.

RUN FOR YOUR LIFE!

A wildfire can spread at a speed of 14 MPH (23 kmh)—that's faster than most people can run. Many large mammals can outrun the flames, unless they are overcome by smoke. Small or young animals are at a greater risk of dying as the fire spreads.

BAD, BUT ALSO GOOD

Fires create pollution, releasing clouds of soot and greenhouse gases into Earth's atmosphere. However, blazes form a vital part of many natural ecosystems. Many forests and grasslands rely on a fire every so often to clear away thick underbrush.

Wildfires occur on every continent except Antarctica.

About four out of five forest fires are started by people.

Large wildfires generate hurricane-force winds.

FIRE TRIANGLE

A fire has three ingredients, without which it won't burn: fuel, heat, and oxygen. They often are imagined as the three sides of a triangle. Remove one side, and the triangle collapses—the fire dies. This is what firefighters aim to achieve when battling blazes. Fire breaks starve flames of fuel; water takes the heat out of a fire; and fire-retardant foam smothers a fire, starving it of oxygen.

OXYGEN   HEAT

FUEL

FIRESEEKER

While most living things flee from flames, fire-chaser beetles head toward them. These bugs lay their eggs in freshly burned tree trunks and can sense a fire's infrared radiation from 80 miles (130 km) away.

IT'S A TWISTER!

DARK CLOUDS BUNCH OVERHEAD . . . THE WIND PICKS UP . . . THE SKY LOOKS OMINOUS . . . IT'S TORNADO TIME! TWISTERS ARE WHIRLING BEASTS THAT REACH DOWN FROM THE CLOUDS.

Twisters are violent storms. These rapidly twirling tubes of air reach down from storm clouds. Where they touch the ground, they tear across the land. High winds cause massive damage, flinging cars around like leaves and ripping apart houses.

Although some twisters hang around for more than an hour, most are finished within 10 minutes.

TORNADO BREEDERS

Tornados form out of huge "supercell" thunderstorms. These powerful storm clouds reach a towering 50,000 ft (15,240 m) into the sky. They produce funnel clouds that signal the birth of a twister.

Howling tornado winds can reach speeds of 300 MPH (480 kmh).

NOT TOO HOT, NOT TOO COLD

The formation of funnels is driven by the temperature difference between air inside the cloud and the air outside the cloud. Swirling updrafts of warm, moist air are tightly focused by cool, dry air wrapping around them. Just like Goldilocks in the fairy tale with the three bears, the air temperature needs to be "just right." Too hot or too cold, and the swirling tubes of cloud collapse back into themselves.

TORNADO ALERTS

TORNADO WATCH: Conditions are right for a tornado.

TORNADO WARNING: A twister has been sighted.

The 2011 Super Outbreak was the largest and costliest tornado outbreak in US history. In April alone, 362 tornadoes swept across the southeastern states.

Tornados move unpredictably across the ground at speeds of around 30 MPH (48 kmh).

TORNADO ALLEY

The area of the southern plains known as Tornado Alley covers 15 percent of United States territory, but claims almost 30 percent of the country's tornadoes.

States most affected by tornadoes in this region: Texas, Kansas, Oklahoma, Nebraska, Illinois, Colorado, Iowa, Missouri, and Mississippi

DEADLY NATURE

PLANTS AND ANIMALS BRISTLE WITH SO MANY WICKED WEAPONS AND DEADLY DEFENSES, IT ALMOST MAKES STAYING INSIDE SEEM LIKE A GOOD IDEA! MAKE A MENTAL NOTE TO AVOID THESE MOST POWERFUL VENOMS AND TOXINS.

DEATH-STALKER SCORPION

The deathstalker scorpion lives in the deserts of the Middle East. It uses venom stored in its tail to paralyze predators. It strikes swiftly, at up to 51 in (130 cm) per second.

DID YOU KNOW?

Many creatures that are prey for venomous animals have developed immunity to their bites. Mice, squirrels, and hedgehogs survive snakebites that would kill humans.

CONE SNAIL

The geography cone snail's beautiful shell hides a terrible secret: Its teeth are sharp enough to go through a wetsuit and its venom can be fatal to humans.

TAIPAN SNAKE

Australia's inland taipan holds the record for most venomous snake. A single bite delivers enough venom to kill 250,000 mice. Luckily, the snake lives in the remote central deserts and is pretty shy.

PUFFERFISH

Thin slices of raw pufferfish are considered a treat in Japan. Unfortunately, this swimming balloon contains tetrodotoxin. If not prepared properly, this supper will be your last! The blue-ringed octopus—one of the world's most venomous animals—also carries this deadly venom.

CASTOR OIL BEAN

One of the world's nastiest poisons comes from the castor oil bean. Refined from the bean's fibers, a quantity weighing about the same as a grain of salt is enough to kill you if ingested or swallowed.

POISON DART FROG

South American Indians paint the tips of their blowpipe darts with a poison taken from the skin of tiny tree frogs. A dose of batrachotoxin, no bigger than two grains of table salt, is fatal. Poison dart frogs are brightly colored to warn predators that they are not safe to eat.

VENOMOUS VS. POISONOUS

Both venoms and poisons are toxic. Neither is worse than the other. The difference is how each is delivered. A venom is injected into a victim through a bite or sting. A poison is absorbed into the body through the skin, or when eaten. Animals are often venomous, while plants tend to be poisonous.

MOST DEADLY

KILLER BACTERIA

The most toxic substance found in nature is made by microbes. Just one nanogram of botulinum for every 2 lb (1 kg) of weight is fatal for humans. In (very) small doses, the toxin paralyzes muscles. This is why it is used for Botox injections, which "freeze" the face and temporarily prevent wrinkles from showing.

MONSTER WAVE

SPEEDING ACROSS THE OCEAN, A TSUNAMI IS A SERIES OF MAMMOTH WAVES THAT CAUSE DEVASTATION WHEN THEY HIT LAND. KILLER WAVES BATTER THE COAST, HAMMERING BUILDINGS FLAT AND THROWING BOATS AND DEBRIS MILES INLAND.

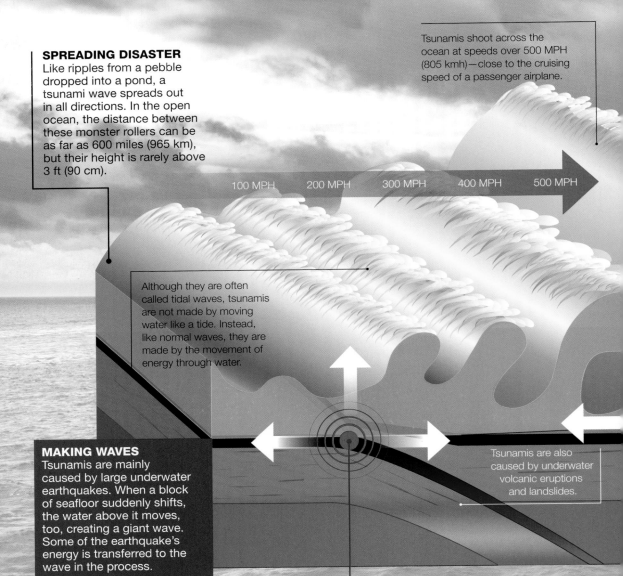

SPREADING DISASTER
Like ripples from a pebble dropped into a pond, a tsunami wave spreads out in all directions. In the open ocean, the distance between these monster rollers can be as far as 600 miles (965 km), but their height is rarely above 3 ft (90 cm).

Tsunamis shoot across the ocean at speeds over 500 MPH (805 kmh)—close to the cruising speed of a passenger airplane.

100 MPH   200 MPH   300 MPH   400 MPH   500 MPH

Although they are often called tidal waves, tsunamis are not made by moving water like a tide. Instead, like normal waves, they are made by the movement of energy through water.

MAKING WAVES
Tsunamis are mainly caused by large underwater earthquakes. When a block of seafloor suddenly shifts, the water above it moves, too, creating a giant wave. Some of the earthquake's energy is transferred to the wave in the process.

Tsunamis are also caused by underwater volcanic eruptions and landslides.

CHRISTMAS CATASTROPHE

The 2004 Indian Ocean earthquake created the world's deadliest tsunami. Nearly one-quarter of a million people died and almost two million people were made homeless. The waves pounded 14 countries, including Indonesia, Sri Lanka, India, and Thailand. It even traveled 3,000 miles (5,000 km) to Africa.

WATER WALL

When a wave reaches land, it slows down and bunches up as the depth becomes shallower. The monster wave now rears up into a wall of water that can be 100 ft (30 m) high—as tall as a 10-story building.

DID YOU KNOW?

Tsunami (say "tsoo-nah-mee") is Japanese for "harbor wave."

Up to 100 ft

RUN-UP

If the trough of a tsunami wave hits the coast first, the water retreats as if it is being sucked out to sea. Harbors can drain and the sea disappears from beaches. The wave hits about five minutes later.

WORLD'S MOST DANGEROUS

WHICH ANIMAL IS THE MOST FEARSOME? HERE'S A ROUNDUP OF THE WORLD'S NASTIEST, DEADLIEST CREATURES, TOGETHER WITH ESTIMATES OF THE NUMBER OF DEATHS THEY CAUSE EACH YEAR.

BRAZILIAN WANDERING SPIDER

Known as the banana spider, this has the most potent venom of all spiders. It loves hiding inside shoes, dark cupboards, cars . . . and bananas, and bites more humans than any other spider.

FEWER THAN 10 (EVER)

BOX JELLYFISH

This tiny jellyfish is a contender for the world's most venomous beast. Its sting is so overpowering, shocked victims drown or suffer heart attacks. Unless treated quickly, there is no hope of survival.

100

HIPPO

Forget lions and tigers, hippos are the world's most dangerous large land mammals. These chubby river horses may look cute, but they are very grumpy. They defend their patch of river with their sharp teeth and 6,000-lb (2,720 kg) bulk.

500

WORLD'S MOST DANGEROUS PLANT

The unassuming little tobacco plant is the world's biggest killer. Nicotine found in the leaves is highly addictive. Despite being poisonous, vast quantities of tobacco are consumed by humans, and it causes more than five million deaths every year.

Crocodile jaws are so strong, they can easily crunch through an arm or a leg!

CROCODILE

These prehistoric top predators eat whatever meat comes their way—fresh or stinky rotten—and some can guzzle over half their body weight in a single sitting. As well as chomping people, one crocodile can even eat another crocodile!

1,000

SNAKES

While not as venomous as many other snakes, the saw-scaled viper is the world's deadliest serpent. It is responsible for around 5,000 of the 50,000 human deaths by snakes every year, mainly because it lives near people and is quick to strike.

100,000

HUMANS

People are their own worst enemy. Worldwide, we are responsible for nearly half a million homicides of our own kind.

437,000

MOSQUITO

The most dangerous of all animals is the mosquito. Diseases transmitted by these pests kill nearly three-quarters of a million people every year! They pass malaria to 200 million people annually. Other mosquito-borne tropical illnesses include Zika virus, dengue fever, and yellow fever.

725,000

GLOSSARY

Alchemist
An early chemist. Alchemists loved magic and potions, and invented many techniques of modern chemistry.

Antifreeze
A substance with a low freezing point that, when mixed with another liquid, lowers the temperature at which the mix freezes.

Bedrock
The solid rocks that underlie the loose soil on Earth's surface.

Buoyancy
The upward force from water that makes things float.

Camouflage
The natural coloring of an animal's skin or fur that helps it blend in with its surroundings.

Carbon dioxide
A colorless, odorless gas produced by an animal's body as a waste product and by burning fossil fuels. Because it absorbs infrared radiation, it traps heat in the atmosphere and is a major contributor to global warming.

Carnivoran
A member of a large and varied group of meat-eating mammals, including cats, dogs, seals, bears, and weasels.

Carnivore
Any meat-eating animal that feeds on other animals.

Cellulose
The tough, woody material that stiffens the walls of a plant's body cells.

Colony
A social group of animals that live together. Animals that live in colonies include ants, bees, and meerkats.

Continent
A large area of dry land.

Electric field
The electrically charged region of space surrounding an electrically charged body.

Emissions
The amount of greenhouse gases produced by a vehicle or activity, or released when making a product.

Facsimile
An exact copy of something.

Fire-retardant
A material that resists burning and stops fire spreading.

Flying buttress
A slanted, arching column that supports a wall.

Galaxy
A vast system of billions of stars, gas, and dust in space.

Global warming
An increase in the planet's temperature, caused by greenhouse gases.

Greenhouse gas
A gas in the atmosphere that traps heat. Carbon dioxide, methane, and nitrous oxide are all greenhouse gases.

Immunity
The ability of a living thing to resist infections or toxins.

Infrared light
Electromagnetic radiation with less energy than visible light. All living things release infrared radiation, which we feel as heat.

Landfall
To arrive on land.

Ligament
A strong, stretchy tissue in the body that connects the bones together.

Magnetic field
A region around a magnet or a moving electric charge that pulls on magnetic materials and charged particles.

Mammal
A warm-blooded vertebrate that suckles its young on milk.

Marsupial
A mammal that raises its very small young inside a pouch.

Microgravity
The experience of weightlessness on board an orbiting spacecraft.

Microorganism
A microscopic living thing, often just one cell. Also known as a microbe.

Migration
The seasonal movement of animals from one place to another.

Mollusk
A group of soft-bodied animals, many of which have shells, that live in watery environments. Includes snails, slugs, clams, and squid.

Mortar
A mixture of lime cement, sand, and water used to bind bricks together.

Neotropical
The tropical regions of Central and South America.

Neutron star
A super-compressed star formed from the core of an older star and composed of neutrons.

Nutrients
Food that provides essential material for growth and overall good health.

Omnivore
An animal that eats both other animals and plants.

Oxygen
A colorless, odorless gas that animals breathe in and use to power chemical reactions in their cells.

Permafrost
A thick layer of soil that stays frozen the whole year round.

Plankton
Tiny plants, animals, and algae floating in seawater or fresh water. Many of these critters are larval stages of larger animals.

Pollution
Damaging substances released into an environment.

Predator
An animal that hunts and kills other animals.

Prey
An animal hunted and killed by other animals.

Radiation
Energy transmitted as electromagnetic waves. Do not confuse with nuclear radiation, which is released when radioactive atomic nuclei break down.

Rain shadow
An area sheltered from rain by a range of hills.

Serrated
Something that has a sawtooth edge, such as a shark's teeth.

Subtropical
Regions close to the tropics.

Synthetic
An artificial, human-made substance.

Tectonic plate
A gigantic, solid slab of rocks that makes up Earth's surface.

Temperate
A region that has mild climate and temperatures.

Tundra
A flat, treeless permafrost plain in the Arctic.

Ultrasonic
Sounds above the range of human hearing.

Ultraviolet (UV) light
Electromagnetic radiation with more energy than visible light. UV from the sun causes sunburn and damages skin.

Updraft
A current of air moving upward.

Vertebrate
An animal that has a backbone.

INDEX

PICTURE CREDITS